London's Lost Route to
MIDHURST

An Historical Account of the Earl of Egremont's Navigation

and the Building of the Petworth Canal

QUEENHITHE *Wharf,*
UPPER THAMES STREET.

SEWARD & Co.'s
Canal Barges
LOAD EVERY
Wednesday and Saturday,
FOR

ARUNDEL,
CHICHESTER, WORTHING,

Amberley	Billingshurst	Emsworth	Little Hampton	Petworth	Steyning
Angmering	Bognor	Havant	Midhurst	Pulbro'	Yapton

and all adjacent and intermediate Places.

ALSO **REGULAR BARGES** TO

Henley, Marlow, Newbury,
Benson, & Wallingford.

The Wharfingers and Proprietors of these Barges not accountable for any Damage by Fire or Water; for River Piracy, of small Parcels above the Value of Five Pounds, unless paid for accordingly; nor for Packages improperly packed, directed, marked, or described; or Leakage arising from bad Casks or Cooperage.

Randell, Howell & Randell, *Wharfingers, &c.*

It is particularly requested that the Gross Weight of all heavy Goods be specified in the Carman's Note.

Wharfage

Received by

Freight

☞ Please to send the Wharfage with your Goods.

TEW, Printer, 34, Queen-street, Cheapside, London.

Seward & Co. of Arundel advertised a twice–weekly service by barge from London to Pulborough, Petworth and Midhurst, 1840.

London's Lost Route to MIDHURST

AN HISTORICAL ACCOUNT OF THE EARL OF EGREMONT'S NAVIGATION AND THE BUILDING OF THE PETWORTH CANAL

P.A.L. VINE

Heedless of pomp, to art and science dear,
Lord of the soil, see EGREMONT appear;
Firm in attachment to his native land,
No foreign feeling guides his fostering hand;
In judgement sound, in contemplation calm,
To gifted Britain still he gives the palm;
To pining genius still he points the way,
And merit ushers to the blaze of day.

SUTTON PUBLISHING

First published in the United Kingdom in 1995 by
Alan Sutton Publishing Ltd · Phoenix Mill · Far Thrupp · Stroud
Gloucestershire

British Library Cataloguing in Publication Data

A catalogue record for this book is available from the British Library.

ISBN 0-7509-0968-4

Typeset in 11/12pt Bembo.
Typesetting and origination by
Alan Sutton Publishing Limited.
Printed in Great Britain by
 WBC, Bridgend, Mid Glam.

This book is dedicated to
the memory of
the men who built the Rother Navigation
in fair weather and foul between 1791 and 1795.

A N

A   C   T

T O

Enable the Earl of *Egremont* to make
and maintain the River *Rother* navigable, from the Town of *Midhurst,*
to a certain Meadow, called the
Railed Pieces, or *Stopham* Meadow, in
the Parifh of *Stopham,* and a naviga-
gable Cut, from the faid River, to
the River *Arun,* at or near *Stopham*
Bridge, in the County of *Sussex;*
and for other Purpofes.

31 *Geo.* III.

[1791.]

Title page of the Rother Navigation Act, 1791.

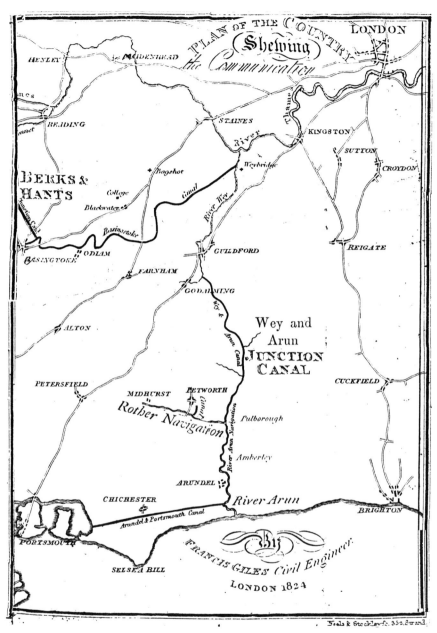

Part of the 1824 Plan by Francis Giles indicating the water route from London to Midhurst.

CONTENTS

Also by P.A.L. Vine

London's Lost Route to the Sea (1965), David & Charles
London's Lost Route to Basingstoke (1968), David & Charles and A.M. Kelly, New York
The Royal Military Canal (1972), David & Charles
Magdala (1973), E.T.O., Addis Ababa
Ethiopia (1974, limited edition), published privately
Introduction to Our Canal Population: George Smith (1974), E.P. Publishing
Pleasure Boating in the Victorian Era (1983), Phillimore
West Sussex Waterways (1985), Middleton Press
Surrey Waterways (1987), Middleton Press
Kent & East Sussex Waterways (1989), Middleton Press
Hampshire Waterways (1990), Middleton Press
London to Portsmouth Waterway (1994), Middleton Press
London's Lost Route to Basingstoke (1994), new edition, Alan Sutton Publishing

LIST OF ILLUSTRATIONS AND MAPS

MAPS

CHRONOLOGICAL TABLE

c. 1560	River Rother navigable to Fittleworth.
1783	William Jessop's first survey of the River Rother.
1785	Arun Navigation Act passed.
1787	Arun Canal opened to Newbridge.
1790	Hardham Tunnel completed.
1791	Rother Navigation Act passed.
1792	Rother Navigation opened to Fittleworth.
1793	Rother Navigation opened to Coultershaw.
1794	Rother Navigation opened to Midhurst.
1795	Petworth Canal opened.
1800	Rotherbridge demolished.
1804	Pallingham Docks built.
1813	Wey & Arun Junction Canal Act passed.
1816	Wey & Arun Junction Canal opened.
1822	Chichester and Portsea ship canals opened.
	Central arch of Stopham Bridge raised.
1823	Portsmouth & Arundel Canal completed.
	William Cobbett notices Coultershaw Wharf.
1826	Petworth Canal closed.
1837	Death of the 3rd Earl of Egremont.
1858	Peak traffic on the Rother Navigation.
1859	Railway from Horsham to Pulborough and Petworth opened.
1863	Railway opened between Hardham and Ford.
1866	Railway opened from Petworth to Midhurst.
1871	Wey & Arun Junction Canal closed.
1888	Arun and Rother navigations closed.
1908	P. Bonthron boats down the River Rother.
1936	Warrant of Abandonment issued for the Rother Navigation.
1955	Pulborough-Midhurst railway closed to passenger traffic.

The 3rd Earl of Egremont, the proprietor of the Rother Navigation, at the age of eighty-three.

PREFACE

On the outskirts of Dunsfold in Surrey I dismounted from my bicycle and plunged into the forest. The Second World War was being waged and I was a schoolboy with a torn paper map trying to locate a wriggly line marked 'old canal'. The discovery of a leaf-covered depression bordered by tree-lined banks winding through Sidney Wood led to one of my life's absorbing interests. Twenty years were to pass before *London's Lost Route to the Sea* was finished. Twenty-five more before this account was completed.

The 3rd Earl of Egremont's enthusiasm for inland navigation had been fired at an early age by the success of the Duke of Bridgewater's canal. Within twenty years of its opening, the young earl was studying how inland navigation could be utilized to improve his estate at Petworth. His interest in water transportation spanned more than twenty years of his life and although his enthusiasm for promoting waterways sometimes lacked financial judgement, his great wealth enabled him to put social benefits before the profit motive.

The Rother Navigation was the first of his waterway adventures and his most successful. This is the story of how the navigation came to be built and how it flourished for the best part of a century. Lord Egremont had hoped to build a direct water link from Petworth to Guildford and the Thames, but in this he was to be disappointed and might have remained so had he not become the leading promoter of the Wey & Arun Junction Canal, whose opening brought Midhurst and Petworth into direct water communication with London and the national network of waterways.

The navigators, the bargemasters, the wharfingers, the toll collector, the maintenance men with the ballast barge, are all shadows of the past coming to life in the neat ink entries of Upton's account books. This book is their memorial and a reminder of a life-style long departed.

It is a simple tale of few incidents but it is unusual in being about one of the few British waterways to be financed and owned by one proprietor. However, whereas much has been written about the Duke of Bridgewater's canal which ushered in the canal era, little has been written about the Earl of Egremont's navigation.

Among the many people who have given me assistance I would particularly thank Lord Egremont for allowing me to study the archives at Petworth House and both Mrs Patricia Gill and Mrs Alison McCann of the West Sussex

Record Office for their assistance. I am also indebted to the 4th Baron Leconfield, Hugh Compton, John Giffin, Gerald Griffith, Charles Hadfield, Dr Richard Pepper, Dr Roger Sellman, the late Francis Steer, 'Jumbo' Taylor, the late Wendy Sawyer and the staff of the West Sussex Record Office for helpful suggestions and advice.

Roger Dunbar, Dendy Easton, Alistair Morris, Brian Perry and Tony Wilsmore provided invaluable help in charting the lower reaches of the river and in sharing the tribulations of portaging craft over stony shallows and around abandoned locks between Midhurst and Pulborough. Paul Locker very kindly arranged for the painting of Fittleworth Wharf to be photographed. M. and R. Carter, Dieter Jebens, Paul Garton, Sotheby's, John Wood and Ian Wright assisted with the illustrations.

I am particularly indebted to both Rosalind and Kay for assisting with the research and typing the manuscript and to Edwina for forbearance in finding that her father's preoccupation with waterways often influenced her recreational pursuits as well as causing her to suffer shipwreck on the upper reaches of the Arun.

P.A.L.V.
St Philip
Barbados
April 1990

CONVERSION TABLES

Imperial to Metric Measurements			Sterling Currency Conversion		
1 inch	=	2.5 cm	One farthing ($^{1}/_{4}d$)	=	0.1p
1 foot	=	30.5 cm	One penny (1d)	=	0.4p
1 yard	=	0.9 m	One shilling (1s)	=	5p
1 furlong	=	201.2 m	Half a crown (2s 6d)	=	12.5p
1 mile	=	1.6 km	One guinea (21s)	=	£1 05p

CHAPTER ONE

THE RIVER ROTHER BEFORE 1791

*The Rother's source – its course – character – navigable to Fittleworth (c. 1560) –
Lord Egremont's interest in improving the river – William Jessop – his early life –
surveys the river from Coultershaw to Pulborough (1783) – The Arun Navigation Act
(1785) – Jessop's survey (1789) and estimate of the cost of making the Rother
navigable to Midhurst (1790) – Lord Egremont's petition for a bill (1791) –
parliamentary proceedings – the Rother Navigation Act (1791).*

The Rother is a softly flowing river in southern England. It rises on the slopes
of Noar Hill, near Selborne in Hampshire, and flows eastwards across Sussex
to form a major tributary of the River Arun below Stopham Bridge. It is
generally known as the Western Rother to avoid confusion with the Eastern
Rother which forms part of the county boundary between Kent and Sussex
and flows into the English Channel at Rye.

The river's early course is enshrouded by undergrowth. Seldom gushing
forth, as when Gilbert White described its course, it trickles down beneath
tangled tunnels of thorn and thicket until it reaches Hawkley Mill Cottages.
Beyond, it flows through a narrow gorge which eventually leads to the
meadowland surrounding Greatham Farm and the bridge carrying the main
road from Petersfield.[1] As the Rother reaches the outskirts of Liss and Sheet
Mill it becomes a sizeable brook, and near the ruins of Durfold Abbey the
fifteenth-century bridge requires four arches to carry pedestrians and traffic.
From here to Midhurst the stream passes through a succession of attractive
villages and hamlets where formerly rose watermills and ancient bridges.[2]
Beyond Terwick Mill and close by the Norman church of Rogate stands
Trotton Bridge, an unusually fine stone example built with five arches in the
fifteenth century. From here an ardent canoeist might in a rainy spell brave the
shallows, shoals, and stony bed of the river to ply his paddle through the trout
pools.★

The Rother skirts the market town of Midhurst and flows through
Cowdray Park, Amersham, Selham, Shopham and Fittleworth to join the tidal

---

★ The 1896 edition of the *Oarsman's Guide* suggested starting from Iping Bridge.

reaches of the Arun a quarter of a mile below Stopham Bridge. For centuries the River Arun was the main artery of commerce in West Sussex; its lower reaches had been used for navigation since the eleventh century and, during the reign of Queen Elizabeth I, the Arun was made navigable from Littlehampton as far as its junction with the Rother at a place called 'turning stream'. The water-bailiff's book, *The High Stream of Arundel*, states that by the beginning of Queen Elizabeth I's reign (1553) the waterway extended as far as Pallingham Quay. It was a slow and at times hazardous navigation involving the passage of twenty-nine crude wooden weirs, or fish kindles, between Houghton and Pallingham, of which fourteen were below Pulborough.

An Amberley court roll of 1615 indicates that Fittleworth Mill was used for making flour and malt and that close to the mill stood a rough wharf supported by timber piles which the miller had to maintain.[3] Therefore some form of navigation probably existed as far as Fittleworth by the latter part of the sixteenth century.

The improvements effected under the Littlehampton Harbour Act of 1732 brought increased trade to Arundel and barges often plied the river up to Pulborough, Fittleworth and Pallingham, but because of the shoals and shallows they could rarely carry more than 15 tons.[4]

It was the decision by a group of merchants, landowners and farmers in the Arun Valley in the early 1780s to do something to improve the navigation above Houghton Bridge that led the 3rd Earl of Egremont to consider whether the Rother might be made navigable as far as Petworth.[5] In the early spring of 1783 he invited William Jessop to survey the river.★

William Jessop (1745–1814) was to become one of the most distinguished canal engineers of his time, and between 1790 and 1806 he was regarded as one of the leading, if not the first, engineer in the kingdom.[6] In 1783 he was on the threshold of his career and it was one of Lord Egremont's characteristics to appreciate and assist promising talent without delay. Jessop had been well grounded in his profession. In 1759, at the age of fourteen, he

---

★ The date of William Jessop's first visit to Petworth may have been sometime during 1780 but it seems unlikely. Among Egremont's papers there is an account from Jessop which reads: 'For two days on a journey to Petworth on a view of the Navigation of the River Rother – ten guineas'. What transpired on this visit is not known and what is surprising is that this account, dated 25 July 1800, was forwarded twenty years after his visit. The account is margined by William Tyler on 26 July 1800, stating that Lord Egremont says it was paid. The lapse in time on Jessop's part can only be accounted for by Lord Egremont querying Jessop's account for his five days' work on the Shoreham Harbour Bill. 'The time from my setting out with your lordship to returning to London, which would have been the time if I had gone specially to Shoreham without visiting Petworth on my way; as your lordship has desired me to make a deduction from the bill which I have sent in, be pleased to desire that the 5 days may be altered to 4.' Jessop's report on Shoreham Harbour is dated 17 July 1800.

was apprenticed to John Smeaton (1724–92) and had continued as his assistant for thirteen years. During this period he gained valuable experience in the science of drainage and canal building, but it was as a river engineer that he came to be best regarded. In 1774 Jessop gave evidence before the parliamentary committee on the Leeds & Selby Canal Bill. After advising on the construction of the Selby Canal, he was appointed engineer to execute the works which were completed in 1778.

Between 1776 and 1783 Jessop advised the committee of the Loughborough, Leicester and Trent Navigations, and it was probably during the parliamentary proceedings of the latter that he came to Lord Egremont's attention. During August and September 1782 Jessop had surveyed 70 miles of the River Trent, seeking a method of improving the navigation without having recourse to locks. The river abounded in shoals and fords, and to overcome these shallows Jessop advocated periodic dredging, deepening a firm bottom and building weirs of piles compounded with faggots bound and covered with willow. He proposed a 30 ft channel and a minimum draught of 18 inches. By the time Jessop appeared before the parliamentary committee in both Houses of Parliament a minimum draught of 21 inches had been agreed. Egremont may well have recognized that the problems of the Trent were not unlike those of the Rother and asked Jessop if he would report on the practicalities of making the river navigable.

When Jessop visited Petworth in April 1783, he was thirty-eight. One can visualize him at Petworth House discussing with the 32-year-old Egremont the viability of waterways and the benefits they could bring to agriculture generally. Egremont would have told him about the proposals to improve the Arun Navigation above Houghton.

The next day, accompanied by the earl's surveyor Thomas Upton, Jessop began the preliminary survey of the river. As they were rowed downstream from Coultershaw, he and Upton studied the banks, carried out soundings, pin-pointed the major shoals, noted the best way to circumvent Fittleworth Mill, and where cuts could most profitably be made through the water meadows to avoid the river's sinuosities.

Jessop's report, dated 16 April 1783, was written from the offices of the Smeatonian Society, Southampton Street, of which he was at that time its Secretary. 'It may be made', he wrote, 'a good navigable river with very little difficulty and at no great expense.' He went on to mention that if the river was a little larger, it might be a 'tolerable' navigation without locks except for passing Fittleworth Mill, but that it was in its natural state too narrow to allow barges to pass each other in dry seasons without additional locks. Although the river fell only 15 ft 6 in between Coultershaw and the Arun at Stopham he had to recommend no less than four locks because the

Portrait of Lord Egremont as a young man, *c.* 1775. (Courtesy of Thos Agnew & Sons Ltd, London)

William Jessop (1745–1814), one of Britain's foremost canal engineers at the age of fifty-one. (Courtesy of the National Portrait Gallery, London)

4

river banks rose only 3 or 4 ft. The cost he thought would be in the region of £4,000.

Jessop pointed out that 'very little wants doing' to the present navigation below Stopham to carry boats of larger burthen. 'I should recommend that instead of 15 tons which the present boats carry, the locks should be made to receive boats of 30 tons.' However, among the items needed to be done was the removal of shallows between Pulborough Bridge.

Egremont studied Jessop's report and waited to see how the proposals to improve the River Arun fared. In February 1784 the petition to the House of Lords stated that the navigation

was much obstructed by shoals and many other impediments and was so shallow in places that it was inconvenient for the carriage of merchandise. The matter was not proceeded with until the following year, when leave

RIVERS ARUN and ROTHER NAVIGATION.

WHEREAS a standing order of the House of Commons directs, that, before any petition is presented to that House, for making a Canal for the purpose of navigation, or for making or improving the navigation of a river, notice of such intended application to parliament, describing the parishes through which the said canal or navigation passes, or is intended to be carried, be printed, in some one newspaper of every and each county through which such canal or navigation passes or is intended to be carried, three times at least, in the months of August and September, or either of them, immediately preceding the session of parliament in which such petition is to be presented: NOTICE IS therefore HEREBY GIVEN,

That a Petition is intended to be presented to Parliament, in their next session, for an Act to make and improve the Navigation of the Rivers ARUN and ROTHER; and to make a canal in and through the several parishes of Amberley, Wiggenholt, Gretham, Pulborough, Hardham, Stopham, Coldwaltham, Fittleworth, Bury, Coates, Egdean, Sutton, Burton, Petworth, Tillington, Duncton, Lodsworth, Selham, Easebourne, Woollavington, and Midhurst, in the county of Sussex, and the tything of South Ambersham, in the parish of Steep, in the county of Southampton.

Notice of petition to House of Commons to build the navigation (*Hampshire Chronicle*, 13 September 1790). The sections relating to the Arun Navigation were deleted before the bill was presented.

was granted to bring in a bill which would improve the navigation above Houghton and authorize the construction of two canals between Coldwaltham and Hardham and between Pallingham and Newbridge wharf. The inhabitants of Pulborough and adjacent parishes protested against the proposed toll to be levied on goods passing between Houghton bridge and Pallingham since no toll was then payable and 'repeated declarations had been made that none was intended to be imposed'. Furthermore, it was claimed that great injury would be caused by the erection of locks and 'no possible advantage could accrue to the petitioners from the extension to Newbridge'. The petitioners won their main point and although the Arun Navigation Act, passed in May 1785, authorized the improvement of the tide-way above Houghton bridge, it specified that the navigation of the river between Houghton and Pallingham was to remain free of toll 'even if locks have to be, in time, erected between Houghton and Greatham Bridge'.

What is not clear is whether Lord Egremont was consulted or had any views regarding the intention of the Arun proprietors to use a stretch of the River Rother to regain entry from the Coldwaltham Cut to the River Arun and to build Hardham Lock.

The Act, inscribed on over 50 ft of vellum, was considerably more specific than many earlier bills. Maximum toll rates were quoted for different items between several places for various quantities. No barge was to pass through any lock with less than ten tons without leave. To prevent impositions by boatmen, maximum freight charges were specified, as well as penalties for overcharging. Concessional rates were granted to barges carrying sea-gravel for the repair of any of the roads leading in the direction of Newbridge wharf. Any damage to the navigation was to be regarded as a felony, but for wilful obstruction the worst fate that could befall an offender was one month in the 'House of Correction'.

The Arun Canal from Pallingham to Newbridge was opened in August 1787 and the Coldwaltham Cut, which enabled barges to avoid the sinuous river channel near Pulborough by passing through Hardham Tunnel, was completed during the summer of 1790. Now was the time for Lord Egremont to go ahead with his own scheme. William Jessop had carried out a further survey of the river from Greatham Bridge to Midhurst in 1789 and estimated the cost of building the navigation from Stopham to Midhurst in March 1790 as £10,373. Jessop expected the traffic to produce a return of between 5 and 7 per cent on this sum, and on 23 August he advised on the procedures to be followed 'if your lordship means to bring in a bill into Parliament this session'.

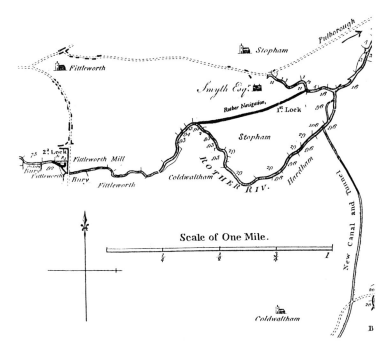

Plan of the Rother Navigation, 1793: (i) Stopham to Fittleworth; the first lock is in the grounds of Stopham House.

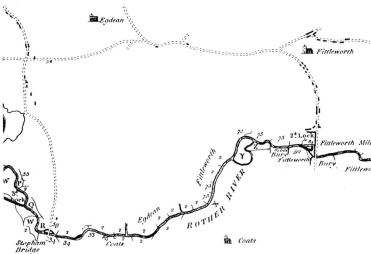

(ii) Fittleworth to Shopham Lock (third); Shopham Bridge is incorrectly named Stopham.

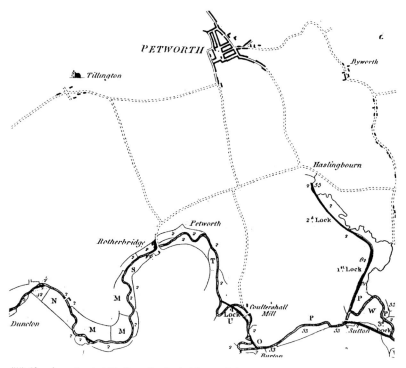

(iii) Shopham Lock (third) to Rotherbridge and the Petworth Canal.

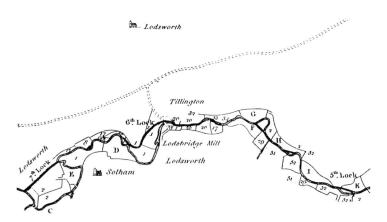

(iv) Ladymead Lock (fifth) to Moorland Lock (seventh); Selham is misspelt.

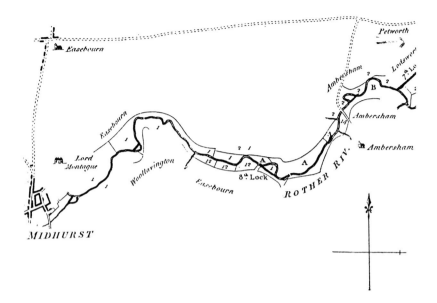

(v) Ambersham to Midhurst; Cowdray House is shown by 'Lord Montague'. The
eighth lock is Todham.

Before a bill could be approved by a parliamentary committee it had to
comply with the standing orders of the House of Commons. One of these
was that every landowner and occupier, whose property adjoined the
proposed line of navigation, needed to be asked whether he assented,
dissented or had no view about its desirability. The 12 miles of navigation
crossed or touched upon sixteen parishes involving 213 properties of which
Lord Egremont owned fifty and Lord Montague fourteen. A total of fifty-four
were owner-occupied and the remainder let to tenants. The first approaches
were made at the end of November 1790, but they were not completed until
three months after the Act had been passed which may indicate why the
standing orders governing private bills were tightened in 1794.[7] According to
the list compiled by Lord Egremont's attorney, no dissents were recorded
although Walter Smyth of Stopham House is not shown as either assenting or
dissenting.

Lord Egremont obtained his Act of Parliament with remarkable speed. He
petitioned the House of Commons for leave to bring in a bill on 16 February
1791; the first reading took place later that month, the second a week later.
The bill was reported with amendments on 16 March and received its third

reading on 21 March – a total of only thirty-three days. The bill was then taken to the House of Lords on 22 March where its three readings were accomplished within seven days. On 11 April the Rother Navigation Act, which ran to forty-two pages, received the royal assent. The preamble stated that the navigation would 'tend to improve the lands and estates adjoining to and near the said intended navigation and will also be of great public utility'. It alluded to the fact that the Earl of Egremont was the proprietor of a very large proportion of the land situated on and near the banks of the river and was willing at his own expense to make and maintain the navigation. It also empowered him to make a canal from Shopham Bridge to Haslingbourne Bridge.* Within 1,000 yards of the river, land and water could be taken, banks raised and trenches dug. All natural impediments to the intended navigation could be removed, mills had to open or shut their sluices as directed to enable a minimum depth of 3 ft 6 in to be maintained. The only limitation was that no land could be taken which on 1 January 1791 was a garden or avenue to a house or lawn 'inclosed and adjoining to a mansion' without the consent of the owners, other than gardens belonging to cottages of less than £6 p.a. value and 'the planted walk and grounds of Lord Viscount Montague'. The remainder of the Act was primarily concerned with the methods to be adopted in determining and paying compensation for damages, and with penalties for anyone poaching or damaging the works.

J. Phillips in the addenda to the 1793 edition of his *General History of Inland Navigation* commented that 'there can be no doubt but the patriotic undertaker of this scheme will not only materially benefit his own lands and estates, but receive the best of thanks from the neighbouring country, for so noble an exertion in the cause of their accommodation'.

Joseph Priestley, whose historical account of navigable rivers in Great Britain was published in 1831, stated that the principal object of the navigation was to supply the interior with coal and to export lead, corn and 'that beautiful variegated fossil limestone, well known in London by the name of Petworth Marble'. However, a curious feature of the Act was the omission of any reference to the Arun Navigation, which barges using the Rother Navigation were bound to use whether proceeding up to Newbridge or down to the sea.

---

* The Act stated 'and likewise to make and maintain one other navigable cut or canal, from the said River Rother, at or near Stopham Bridge to a certain bridge called Haslingbourn Bridge. . . .' Stopham should have read Shopham!

CHAPTER TWO

THE 3RD EARL OF EGREMONT (1751–1837)

His parentage, education and early life – enjoys feminine companionship – becomes disenchanted with politics – retires to Petworth – eventual marriage (1801) and separation – his children – Egremont's interest in improving his estate – becomes a successful stock breeder – studies agriculture – invites Arthur Young to Petworth (1793) – also William Jessop – Egremont's leisure activities – patron of the arts – relationship with J.M.W. Turner – John Constable – Egremont's benevolent disposition – hospitality – eccentricities – declining years and death – obituary.

George O'Brien Wyndham, the 3rd Earl of Egremont, was born on 18 December 1751. He was a remarkable man even in an age which produced many men of innovative and eccentric character. Indeed, it is surprising in view of the diversity of his achievements that no biography has yet been published. His titles include: peer of the realm, Lord Lieutenant of Sussex (1819–35), Colonel of the Sussex Regiment, Commissioner of the Port of Arundel and of Shoreham Harbour; he was sole proprietor of the Rother Navigation, farmer *par excellence*, cattle breeder, racehorse owner, innovator, entrepreneur, patron of the arts, philanthropist and sportsman.

Details of his life are mainly garnered from snippets of gossip or eulogies from house-guests, many of whom were too much in awe of his wealth to challenge his conceits or scoff at his oddities. He appeared to have had few intimate friends and his closest acquaintances were those whose interests he shared. He took no prominent part in politics; however, he listened to the Earl of Chatham (Pitt the Elder) protesting against the government's policy towards the American colonists and witnessed the famous death scene on 7 April 1778. In 1782 he preferred to be at the House than watching his first Derby winner. However, after William Pitt (the Younger) became prime minister (1783) his appearances in the House of Lords were rare as he disliked Pitt and mistrusted his colleagues. Yet statesman Charles James Fox⋆ (1749–1806) declared he valued Egremont's opinion on his India bill, 1783,

---

⋆ Fox was MP for the pocket borough of Midhurst (1768–74). Stanley Ayling's recent biography (1990), however, makes no mention of his relationship with Egremont.

more than that of any other man, and Charles Greville★ (1794–1865) felt he might have played a conspicuous part in government. In 1792 the split in the Whig party over the French Revolution occurred and Egremont crossed over to support Pitt's proclamation against wicked and seditious writings. In 1820, after Prime Minister Lord Liverpool introduced a bill to deprive Her Majesty Queen Caroline of her title and to dissolve her marriage to King George IV, Egremont attended the trial in the House of Lords. Although the bill passed its second reading by 123 votes to 95, many peers, including Egremont, felt that the monarch was as guilty of indiscretions as his consort.[8]

In 1750 his father, Sir Charles Wyndham, had inherited the earldom from his uncle, the 7th Duke of Somerset, and in 1761 he had replaced William Pitt the Elder (Earl of Chatham) as Secretary of State for the southern department. In the short time that the 2nd earl held office (he died in 1763) he was much involved in negotiating the terms of the peace treaty to end the Seven Years War (1756–63), but he was by all accounts a much less able man than his counterpart, George Grenville, Secretary for the northern department. Indeed, historians have yet to say much in his favour. Ronald Hyam concluded that 'he was dull and dry, uninventive and narrow-minded, ungracious and malicious, greedy and probably corrupt, and far from disinterested'.[9]

George Wyndham was eleven and a half years old when he succeeded to the title. He was educated at Westminster where he showed an aptitude for the classics and the arts. In June 1767 his mother Alicia Mary (1729–94) remarried Count von Bruhl, a diplomat from Saxony. In 1770, soon after leaving school, the 3rd earl made a grand tour of Europe lasting five months. For the remainder of the decade he spent much of his time enjoying a lively social life in London, and female companionship in particular. In a letter to Lord Holland he described the society into which he entered when he came of age in 1772: 'Voltaire and Rousseau were both alive and their art and their doctrines engrossed the attention of everybody . . . everything in fashionable life, dress, food, amusement, morals and manners, all must be French . . . there was hardly a young lady of fashion who did not think it almost a stain on her reputation if she was not known to have cuckolded her husband.'[10] In London (Egremont remembered walking in the Mall of a Sunday evening in full dress coat, bag and sword, with chapeau-bras under his arm) Fox was a close friend and racing companion to whom he lent or gave many hundreds of pounds to settle gambling debts.† Georgiana, Duchess of Devonshire, was

---

★ The celebrated diarist who was clerk to the Privy Council (1821–59).

† It was said of Fox that in spite of great pecuniary distress, he refused to be bribed by the emoluments of office.

another grateful borrower: 'My dearest Lord Egremont. I write from Chiswick where I am very desirous to stay but alas unless you can for this once exert yourself for me, I must return to town tonight. If you have the goodness to post me a draft for £300 tomorrow in a blank cover, it will enable me to spend two more days here.'[11] This draft was sent and a second letter from her requested the repayment date to be postponed.

In 1778 Egremont visited Portsmouth where the king was reviewing the fleet. 'I went with a party, one of which was a lady with whom I was very much in love, without her husband, and living in the same lodging with her.' He was also invited to dine with George III after the review, 'a thing unknown in those days', but this exploit was suddenly interrupted; 'I abandoned review, mistress and King and went post to the House of Lords' to oppose a private bill concerning a friend.[12]

Until the age of thirty Egremont was very much the man about town, wearing sumptuous apparel at court balls and seeking the company of beautiful and interesting women. He was a rival of the Duc de Chartres for the favours of the courtesan Mademoiselle Duthe, to whom he gave a gilt coach and who was observed 'all bediamonded' in his box at the opera. He had a close friendship with Lady Melbourne, wife of the prime minister,* and became her lover in around 1778. However, his amorous intrigues ceased, at least temporarily, when he became engaged to Lady Maria Waldegrave, a stepdaughter of the Duke of Gloucester and great-granddaughter of Sir Robert Walpole. Everyone favoured the match except Maria's mother, who never liked him; Egremont too began to get cold feet. He increasingly found court life tedious and his natural shyness caused him to shrink from marriage and from the metropolis. Maria doubtless found Egremont hard to understand. Their relationship was not altogether happy and after he had resumed his liaison with Lady Melbourne, they parted. As Lady Sarah Lennox wrote, 'she did it like an angel and without reproach'. Egremont was reputed to be the father of William Lamb, afterwards 2nd Viscount Melbourne, who had been born in March 1779.†

In the early 1780s Lord Egremont withdrew from the London scene and increasingly spent more time at Petworth. About 1784 he became enamoured with a teenage girl, Elizabeth Iliffe (1769–1822), whose parentage remains obscure. Her father is thought to have been either a clergyman at Westminster

---

* Lord Melbourne was twice prime minister, in 1834 and 1835–41.

† The young Melbournes came regularly to Petworth to play in the gardens and view the Arab horses, and later, when Home Secretary (1830–4), William was a frequent visitor who delighted in the old man's conversation.

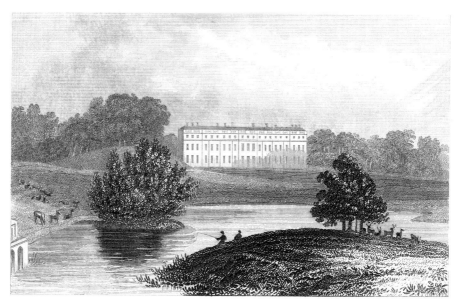

Petworth House, the seat of the Earl of Egremont, 1821. The boathouse on the lake can be seen in the left-hand corner. The park was landscaped by Lancelot 'Capability' Brown (1715–83) in the 1750s.

School or a Devonshire farmer. It seems to have been a union of real affection – she took great delight in painting and shared the earl's artistic tastes – though not of exclusive devotion, because there was a contemporary liaison with Elizabeth Fox who bore him four children in the 1790s. Not until 16 July 1801, by which time he was fifty and Elizabeth Ilive had borne him seven children, were they married privately at Petworth. But the marriage that should have established her position, destroyed it; in May 1803 she went to live in London and made only rare visits to Petworth.★ A daughter, Elizabeth, who died in infancy (1803), was the only product of the lawful union. Although his eldest son George, who took the name Wyndham by royal licence, inherited the greater part of his estates, the earl's irregular

★ 'Mrs Wyndham was married to Lord Egremont about two years ago. He believes she was a farmer's daughter and was with his Lordship at fifteen years of age. She was according to her own account neither desirous of being married to his Lordship nor of being acknowledged Countess of Egremont and he said she might declare herself if she pleased. The cause of their present unhappiness is jealousy on her part. She apprehends his Lordship is not faithful to her and that with people about her; at present they do not cohabit.' (*The Diary of Joseph Farington*, vol. II, 9 October 1803 (*The Farington Diary*, ed. James Greig, 6 vols, 1922–6)) relationships, common as they were at that period among the aristocracy, must have caused much ill feeling in the family. Contemporaries, however, accepted Egremont's liaisons with tolerant reserve. There were numerous connections of this kind recorded in the eighteenth century and some, like that of Lavinia Fenton (the Polly of the *Beggar's Opera*) who lived with the Duke of Bolton, were celebrated. Creevey, staying at Petworth in 1828, was shown the paintings. "In reply to a question about a coach and six, Egremont replied, 'Ah! It is a devilish clever picture, is it not? Let's go look at it,' and so they did. He then fixed his eyes on a portrait of a lovely woman. 'Did you ever see a handsomer face than that?' 'Never,' say I, 'by whom was it done?' 'By Sir Joshua Reynolds,' says he, and he stood still looking at it. I, at length said 'Whose picture is it, Lord Egremont?' 'Oh,' he said, 'it was a lady not much known in the world,' and he turned away."[13] Indeed so numerous were the women in Egremont's life that it is difficult to fit them into an accurate chronology. Egremont's own children must have found the family situation particularly difficult, not only after their father had married, but during the succeeding years. As Lady Spencer told Lady Bessborough in 1813:

> nothing will persuade her that Lord Egremont has not forty-three children who all live in the house with him and their respective mothers, that the latter are usually kept in the background, but that when any quarrels arise, which few days pass without, each mother takes part with her progeny, bursts into the drawing room, fights with each other, Lord Egremont and his children, and I believe the Company, and make scenes worthy of Billingsgate or a Mad House.[14]

C.R. Leslie, who stayed at Petworth every year between 1826 and 1837, remarked upon Egremont's affection for children and on how his grandchildren were brought into his room in the morning while he was dressing.[15] Greville noted that he was passionately fond of children and that animals of every description found favour in his sight. In September 1805 he even hired a boat so that his family could see Nelson join the fleet at Portsmouth.

The diversity of Lord Egremont's activities was extremely wide. His interests in horse-racing, cattle breeding, agriculture, harbour improvements and water transport were all linked to the improvement of his estates, while his enthusiasm for art, literature and science, coupled with his love for the countryside, filled his leisure hours. Greville wrote that he preferred to revel unshackled in all the enjoyments of private life, both physical and intellectual, which an enormous fortune, a vigorous constitution, and literary habits placed in abundant variety before him.[16] One of his first projects in the 1780s was to turn the large parklands adjoining the house to agricultural use:

Previously to its being improved, it was an entire forest scene, oversowed with bushes, furze, some timber, and rubbish; of no kind of use, if we except a few miserable and ragged stock which it annually reared; and would not have lett (sic) for more than 4s or at most 5s per acre. The undertaking of converting between 700 and 800 acres of land was an exertion to be expected only from an animated and enlightened improver. It was begun about sixteen or seventeen years ago;★ the timber sold, the underwood grubbed, and burned into charcoal upon the spot; and every aspect of the park has been since drained in the most effectual manner: the whole of it enclosed and divided into proper fields.[17]

William Marshall (1745–1818) noted the superiority of Petworth cattle as a result of Egremont's efforts to improve breeding.[18] In addition to offering an annual prize at Petworth Fair for the finest bull and heifer, Egremont established a society at Lewes in 1797 for the improvement of cattle. In his own park the herd of deer numbered 512 at the time of his death, while Thomas Philip's view of 'Petworth Park' in 1798 gives an impressive view of the diversity of livestock, which included flocks of various breeds of sheep and pigs.

Horse breeding as well as stock breeding was one of Egremont's keen interests. For many years he maintained a racing stud which was remarkably successful. 'Nimrod', writing in 1837, regarded him as 'one of the main contributors to the legitimate end of racing – the improvement of the breed of horses – his lordship having always paid regard to what is termed stout or honest blood'.[19] Lord Egremont bred five Derby winners (Assassin 1782, Hannibal 1804, Cardinal Beaufort 1805, Election 1807, Lapdog 1826) and seven runners-up (1793, 1794, 1795, 1799, 1800, 1806, and 1812) as well as five winners of the Oaks.

Gohanna, Derby runner-up in 1793 and sire of Cardinal Beaufort and Election, was named after a hill near which he was foaled and by which the proposed extension of the Petworth Canal would have passed; in 1795 Egremont's Arun started favourite in the Derby but finished near the tail-end of the field.[20] Lapdog, only a moderate racehorse, started at 50–1 and won on an appallingly wet day. His last Derby runner was Hock which started at 30–1 in 1836. In later years Egremont's interest in racing waned. Creevey inspected the stud in 1828 and heard his lordship observe that he wasn't much interested

---

★ In other words about 1780. Although the Revd Arthur Young's report was not published until 1808, much of it was written about 1795 and added to each year until 1799. The only later additions to the text were statistics about sheep.

Arthur Young, the celebrated agriculturist
(1741–1820), *c.* 1790.

'in the thing' and that it had been an amusement for his brother Charles. Many years before, this brother had cost him dear; between two and three hundred thousand pounds apparently. In 1832 the stud groom told Greville that there were three hundred horses in the stables. Nimrod commented that Lord Egremont had received great assistance from his late brother since whose decease (in 1828) the stable had not been so successful. It was Egremont's decision to abandon the regular race meetings in Petworth Park which led the 3rd Duke of Richmond to establish the Goodwood meetings in 1801.

Many of Lord Egremont's farming practices were recorded by Arthur Young (1741–1820) and his son, the Revd Arthur Young★ (1769–1827) as well as by William Marshall who stayed at Petworth in 1791.† Betham-

★ The Revd Arthur Young was educated at Eton before taking Holy Orders; he married Jane Berry in 1799. In 1802 the Committee of the Board of Agriculture voted him £50 for 'his labour in arranging during 13 weeks the "Reports from Enclosed Parishes to the House of Commons"'. In 1805 he went to Moscow with his wife to report on agriculture for the Emperor Alexander and continued to work there until 1814 and from 1815 to 1820. (Betham-Edwardes, *Autobiography of Arthur Young*, 1898, p. 382)

† Marshall gave effusive tributes to Egremont (*The Rural Economy of the Southern Counties*, 1798, vol. 1 p. 45–6), but formally criticized Young junior's report for its many errors and confusions. (Betham-Edwardes, p. 427)

George O'Brien Wyndham seated in the North Gallery at Petworth House at about the time he was drafting the prospectus for the Wey & Arun Junction Canal Company.

Edwardes described the elder Young's life as 'singularly interesting and singularly sad'. Like Egremont he was regarded as an 'untiring experimentalist', who between 1784 and 1809 completed forty-seven volumes on the *Annals of Agriculture*. William Pitt set up the Board of Agriculture in 1793 and Young was chosen as its first Secretary. Young had begun writing about farming in 1767 and four years later wrote his account of 'A Six Weeks Tour of Sussex'. However, when his report on Sussex to the Board of Agriculture appeared in 1793, it made no reference to Petworth. It may have been this omission which resulted in Young being invited down to Petworth in June 1793. Egremont was already familiar with Young's writings and had been introduced to him by Lord Sheffield in December 1792. The visit was a success. Young was prompted to write, 'Pray allow me to express my sincere thanks for the kind reception and valuable information I met at Petworth. I think of it with pleasure and should not feel pleasantly if I did not hope for a renewal of it sometime or other.'[21] Other visits there certainly were and on 31 August that same year Egremont was elected to a seat on the Board of Agriculture.* Between 1793 and 1799 Arthur Young and his son made many trips to Petworth, the results of which are reflected in the revised and much enlarged report on Sussex, which his son had more or less completed by 1797 but which was not published until 1808.

Arthur Young's relationship with Lord Egremont lasted over ten years and their correspondence reveals an easy relationship based on strong mutual interests.[22] In November 1797 he spent an 'interesting, splendid, gay and cheerful week' at Petworth with his son, but could not refrain from commenting that it was 'vain, frivolous and impious'; he also strongly disapproved of the lack of religious feeling; 'in the chapel, no worship, no hats off but my own – dreadful example to a great family and to his children'. However, in spite of his disapproval of the Petworth way of life he appears to have quickly accepted the situation, for six weeks later he is writing 'I have been here above a fortnight. A good deal of rabble, but some better . . . I shall stay the whole vacation.'[23] In 1798 Egremont advised Young over the rumpus caused by his son Arthur writing an ill-advised letter about the O'Connor treason trial at Maidstone, which the Jacobin newspapers assigned to the father in mistake for the son. Young had to write to four papers explaining he was the author.

Many of Young's conversations with Lord Egremont were concerned with the conditions of the poor, and some of Lord Egremont's comments were

---

* The Prime Minister William Pitt offered the post of President to Egremont in 1798, but rather typically he declined it. (Betham-Edwardes, p. 315)

noted in his diary. By 1800 he had become sufficiently well acquainted to write to him: 'I agree with you about the poor and prices and government. They are infatuated but such heads as yours should devise remedies, whether taken or not.'[24] However, on 20 April the following year he had an argument with his lordship at the Farmers' Club over the need for the poor to be given land. Young had probably pushed his views a shade too strongly and it may have been this incident which prompted Lord Egremont to call on him at his home at Bradfield Hall in Berkshire early in May. The only remarks recorded by Young of this meeting was Lord Egremont's comment that the government had gone out of its way in the late debates to abuse the Board of Agriculture.[25] Between the early 1790s and 1801 the price of wheat and barley doubled as it rose to unprecedented heights during the war with France. In May 1802 Egremont, dining at Lord Winchilsea's home in London, told Young that poverty in West Sussex was increasing – 'not a loaf for three days and a half and a mutiny among the Volunteers'.[26] Young's last reference to his meetings with Lord Egremont occurred at the latter's London house in March 1807, although Young continued to assist the Board, even after he became blind in 1810, until 1816 or later.

The canal builder, William Jessop, was another who had close personal contact with Lord Egremont over a period of twenty years. He made numerous visits to Petworth and its vicinity to view the Arun and Rother rivers and to judge the feasibility of linking Petworth to the Wey Navigation. On occasions he also travelled with his lordship to Littlehampton and Shoreham in connection with proposals to improve their harbours. However, their relationship appears to have ceased after Jessop charged for five days work on the Shoreham Harbour Bill which Egremont felt should have been four. After Jessop had amended his fee, he annoyed Egremont by submitting a further account a week later for a visit to Petworth made twenty years before which Egremont said had been paid (see footnote, page 2). On financial matters Egremont was shrewd. Anyone abusing his generosity was given short shrift, as artists who irritated his lordship discovered.

It is evident that Egremont preserved a certain distance between himself and his guests at Petworth – Thomas Daniell, the landscape painter (1740–1840), noted in 1804 that 'there is a great deal of the Peer about him, the effect of a habit of superiority'.[27] The earl also disliked inefficiency and inattention. In December 1816 he wrote to James Dallaway about stupid errors in the first volume of his county history: 'It is really very painful to me to write in a manner that I am afraid will be displeasing to you, but it is necessary to speak the truth.'

Egremont paid great attention to crops, farming implements and machinery. Young relates how detailed experiments were carried out with every variety of vegetables including the cultivation of beans, cabbages, carrots, chicory, lucern, parsnips, potatoes, rhubarb and turnips. The light Suffolk plough was proved superior to the old Sussex wheel-turnrift plough. Other implements introduced were the Suffolk farmer's cart, the mole plough, horse-hoes for beans, iron dibbles (about which Egremont wrote a paper in 1797), scufflers, Mr Ducket's skim-coulters and the Rotherham plough. Typical of the ebullient praise bestowed on his lordship was that of the author of *The Kitchen Garden*, Henry Phillips, who in 1831 dedicated his 'Companion for the Orchard' to 'a nobleman who has so greatly promoted the arts of horticulture and agriculture'.

Many of the experiments were on a grand scale. Not all were successful. A large crop of cabbages planted in the Stag Park at Petworth burst and rotted, but the following year improved draining remedied this loss. In 1797 his lordship produced from his garden for medicinal purposes the largest quantity of opium ever cured in England, and from this it was later concluded that foreign opium was highly adulterated.[28]

Between 1795 and 1796, a period when the price of bread was causing great hardship, Egremont carried out trials by mixing potatoes with wheaten flour to ascertain what proportions gave the best results. He also built a threshing machine at Petworth, one of only three in the county. Young wrote, 'the great attention which the Earl of Egremont has paid in improving the farming implements of Sussex, has already had a considerable effect in the neighbourhood of Petworth, and induced some farmers to adopt the use of those which promise the greatest advantage.[29]

Experiments were carried out with artificial grasses. Many acres were sown. Dutch clover, ray grass and burnet in one field; red clover, ray grass and trefoil in another. To discover whether close cropping was detrimental to the grass, his lordship filled these fields with sheep in autumn and winter and pronounced himself satisfied that this improved the herbage. On a lighter note Young praised the excellent flavour of his lordship's cider, 'the best in Sussex', which was produced on the estate. The engineer John Rennie was another who approved. When writing to William Upton at Petworth in April 1790 about the availability of an oak tree for a client in Leith, he concluded his letter 'when shall I have the cyder?'[30]

Farm buildings were the responsibility of the 'timber surveyor' John Upton, who invented a movable barn floor for threshing corn which was awarded a gold medal and a bounty of thirty guineas by the Royal Society of Arts in 1796. Indeed Young concluded there was 'hardly a suggestion made which had the probability of being turned to improvement which was not acted upon'.

Lord Egremont's leisure activities included hunting, shooting and walking his dogs; there is also some evidence to show that he was interested in boating, both on the lake in Petworth Park and on the Rother. In June 1793 Joseph Muggeridge built a lighter for his lordship. It was 25 ft long and cost £26 5s. It was looked after by William Duff, and was moored below Rotherbridge by Spershotts Hanger and kept in a boathouse built adjacent to Mr Spershotts' orchard. The boat was used by Egremont and Thomas Upton to view progress in building the navigation; it may have been this boat which was sunk in the floods of 1797 and which had to be dragged out of the river by a team of horses. There is also reference to the 'large boat sunk at Rotherbridge' being raised in January 1805 and to three days spent repairing and caulking the 'great boat'. This was probably the boat that was used to take guests to the opening celebration at Midhurst in June 1795. In March 1808 William White had to spend two days refloating the boat after it had sunk again at Rotherbridge.

Sometime prior to 1809 Lord Egremont had the substantial ornamental stone boathouse erected on the northern side of the lake, which is depicted in Turner's oil painting, *Petworth, Sussex, the seat of the Earl of Egremont – Dewy Morning*. In 1817 a new lighter made its appearance and there is reference to William Upton's 'passage boat', which suggests that Lord Egremont probably instigated the building of at least one special craft for the London trade.[31] In September 1822 there is mention of Lucas being sent 'to take my Lord's boat at Coultershaw' and in about 1828 of his lordship sending his hoops to Midhurst on board 'the packet boat'.[32]

Egremont inherited a quantity of antique sculpture and paintings, many still in packing cases, and from this formed a collection for which Petworth House has become justly famous. His patronage was an invaluable support, both morally and financially, to contemporary artists, many of whom rose from obscurity to fame. In 1795 he commissioned Romney to paint Elizabeth Iliffe and his children and in the course of the next forty years sixty-six painters added 263 pictures to his gallery. Thomas Phillips contributed thirty-four, Sir Joshua Reynolds twenty-two, and J.M. Turner twenty; Turner's friendship with Egremont, which lasted from about 1802 until the latter's death, enabled the painter to spend months at Petworth House where he had his own studio, good pike fishing, and the freedom to roam where he wished. While we may regret that Turner did not do for the Rother what Constable did for the Stour, he painted some fine watercolours of the Arun Valley and produced two almost identical paintings of the Chichester Canal.*

---

* One is displayed in the National Gallery, the other at Petworth House. Apparently begun in 1829, it is the only scene to reflect Egremont's canal interests.

It was C.R. Leslie who introduced John Constable, the landscape painter, to Lord Egremont. Constable, after worrying unduly about whether he should write to announce his time of arrival, stayed at Petworth in September 1834. A coach was placed at his disposal and after his visit he wrote that he had 'visited the river banks which are lovely indeed. Claude nor Ruysdad could not do a thousandth part of what nature here presents'.[33] Constable himself sketched the Rother at Cat Hanger, a farm on the Petworth Estate between Lodsbridge and Rotherbridge, but no barges appear in the scene. He also did some drawings of Fittleworth Mill. The following July, while staying with his friend and namesake George Constable at Arundel, he visited Fittleworth twice more. One of his pencil sketches, now in the Victoria & Albert Museum, included a view of the wharf below the bridge showing a moored barge. Constable was enraptured by the beauty of the Sussex countryside. 'I have never seen such scenery as your county affords. I prefer it to any other for my pictures,' he wrote to his friend George. One can only regret that he came to Sussex late in life and that what he saw at Coultershaw could not inspire him to emulate his world-famous pictures of barges and barge-building on the River Stour.

The earl's kindness and extreme modesty endeared him to many. His hospitality was famous. Farington recorded that his lordship lived magnificently. The cuisine at Petworth was good without being ostentatious. Haydon found it plentiful but not absurd profusion. Creevey described it as 'of the first order, turtle, venison, moor game etc. without stint', and when Lord Sefton said, 'This is very good claret, Lord Egremont', Egremont was pleased to reply in his driest manner, 'Is it?' as if he would serve any other to his guests. Rarely did he formally entertain the great, but in June 1814, after the Emperor Napoleon's abdication, he received the Prince Regent, the Tsar of Russia, with his sister the Duchess of Oldenburgh, and the King of Prussia with their suites; the painting *Allied Sovereigns at Petworth* by Phillips depicts the magnificent scene.

The house was run in a fairly disorderly manner like a great inn, especially in Egremont's later days. Everybody came when they thought fit and departed without notice. Breakfast was served from nine to twelve. At six o'clock dinner Egremont met everybody and often did the carving himself for ten or twenty and more. The numerous servants rose early but also went to bed early. In 1828 Creevey described them as 'very numerous tho' most of them advanced in years and tottered, and comical in their looks'. Henry Fox★ wrote in his journal in 1823: 'The want of comforts, of regularity, and still more the

---

★ The son of the nephew of Charles James Fox.

total absence of clean linens, made it, splendid and beautiful as it is, far from being agreeable . . . People of all descriptions without any connections or acquaintance with each other are all huddled up at the dinner table.'[34] Among these people were of course the artists, many of whom were impoverished and found the fare provided excellent. Painter Benjamin Haydon, who stayed in 1826, praised his host's hospitality and added, 'Dogs, horses, cows, deer and pigs, peasantry and servants, guests and family, children and parents, all alike share his bounty and opulence and luxuries'.[35] In December 1832 Greville noted that the house lacks modern comforts and that the hospitality was abundant but not very refined. 'Nimrod' commented on Egremont's liberality in affording the free benefit of several of his stud-horses to his tenantry and neighbours.

Many stories are told of Lord Egremont's kindness and generosity, especially to the estate workers and their families. When times were bad he created employment by ordering improvements to roads in summer[36] or snow clearance in winter. The stone wall, 14 miles in circumference, which girts Petworth Park, remains a testimony to his benevolence. Greville related how every winter Lord Egremont used to feast the poor women and children of the adjoining parishes in the riding house and tennis court, where they were admitted in relays. In 1834 his illness prevented the dinner taking place so the following May it was arranged to hold a fête in the park. Fifty-four tables, each 50 ft long and all laid with cloths, plates and dishes, were placed in a vast semicircle on the lawn before the house.

Two great tents were erected to receive the provisions which were conveyed in carts like ammunition. Plum puddings and loaves were piled like cannon-balls, and innumerable joints of boiled and roast beef were spread out, while hot joints were prepared in the kitchen, and sent forth as soon as the firing of guns announced the hour of the feast. Tickets were given to the inhabitants of a certain district, and the number was about 4,000; but, as many more came, the old peer could not endure that there should be anybody hungering outside his gates, and he went out himself and ordered the barriers to be taken down and admittance given to all. They think 6,000 were fed. Gentlemen from the neighbourhood carved for them, and waiters were provided from among the peasantry. The food was distributed from the tents and carried off upon hurdles to all parts of the semicircle. A band of music paraded round, playing gay airs. The day was glorious – an unclouded sky and soft southern breeze. Nothing could exceed the pleasure of that fine old fellow; he was in and out of the windows of his room twenty times, enjoying the sight of these poor wretches, all attired in their best, cramming themselves and their brats with as much as they could

The 3rd earl's birthday being celebrated in Petworth Park in 1835, from the painting by W.F. Witherington. Lord Egremont is on horseback.

devour and snatching a day of relaxation and happiness. It was altogether one of the gayest and most beautiful spectacles I ever saw.[37]

Witherington's painting of his postponed birthday party was perhaps the most public example of a lifetime's benevolence. However, forty years earlier he had shown his appreciation for the men who had laboured on the Rother Navigation in the vilest of weather by arranging as many as three 'feasts' as each stage was completed. More specifically there are numerous entries of extra payments to sick or injured workmen 'by my lord's order'. One, dated 19 July 1794, shows that Robert Russell, the lock-carpenter, was given two guineas because he was ill and could not work for six weeks. As Burke concluded, Lord Egremont delighted to reign in the dispensation of happiness.

Egremont's quirks have been noted by many observers. One was his inability to remain stationary for more than a moment and his need to be constantly perambulating. Leslie noticed his host's restless disposition and shyness, remarking that after conferring favours Egremont 'was out of the room before there was time to thank him'. He could not bear, wrote Greville in 1832, 'to be personally meddled with, he likes people to come and go as it suits them, and say nothing about it, ever to take leave of him'. Another mannerism was Egremont's dislike of being questioned and his replies were often curt. To encourage his own pet fancies, he allowed his tenants 3 per cent rebate of their annual rent if they used oxen rather than horses for farm work.[38] Consequently the use of teams of oxen to pull ploughs and farm wagons was prolonged in the neighbourhood of Petworth, although their efficacy compared with horses could not be substantiated.

Greville, who visited Petworth two days after Egremont's eighty-first birthday, noted that in spite of his healthy appearance, his course was nearly run.

> He has the mortification of feeling that, though surrounded with children and grandchildren, he is almost the last of his race, and that his family is about to be extinct. Two brothers and one childless nephew are all that are left of the Wyndhams, and the latter has been many years married. All his own children are illegitimate, but he has everything in his power, though nobody has any notion of the manner in which he will dispose of his property.[39]

On 20 June 1837 King William IV died and Queen Victoria ascended the throne. In October the Court moved from Windsor to Brighton for an autumn holiday and Lord Egremont felt obliged to journey there to pay his respects to the new queen. On returning to Petworth 'his old complaint, inflammation of the trachia' laid him low and within a week he was dead, a month before his eighty-sixth birthday. Four days before his demise he completed his will and had various notes of debts burnt in order that those who owed him money need not be troubled. With him at his deathbed was his eldest son George Wyndham.

The funeral took place at Petworth on Tuesday 21 November. As in his lifetime, so at his death, art and land played a leading role. A group of artists, led by Phillips and Turner in their mourning cloaks, included many to whom Egremont had been a friend as well as a patron. Behind the hearse four hundred labourers from the estate walked in pairs, clad in white smocks and black gloves. In addition, local dignitaries, numerous relatives and friends attended the burial, an astonishing testimony to a beloved landlord and one of the great art patrons of all time.

When the news of Egremont's death had just reached him, Greville wrote that 'he was a remarkable man. He was immensely rich and his munificence was equal to his wealth'. Creevey noted that he had settled £40,000 on each of his natural daughters upon their marriage, and that he dealt on the same liberal scale with friends, artists and 'with by no means the least costly customers – with mistresses, of whom Lady Melbourne must have been the most distinguished leader in that way'.[40]

Egremont's public benefactions ranged from supporting public enterprises, like the Brighton Chain Pier and the Portsmouth & Arundel Canal Navigation, to providing horses, uniforms, weapons and equipment for the Petworth Yeomanry. He contributed £20,000 to building the county hospital in Brighton as well as to an infirmary at Chichester; he financed an emigration scheme for the poor of the Petworth area to Canada; in 1793 he built the fine market-house in the town square; he endowed almshouses for twenty poor tradesmen; he repaired Petworth Church including the provision of a steeple. He also ensured that Petworth was one of the first towns in Sussex to have its own water supply and gas works (1836) – twenty-five years before the latter reached Midhurst.

Besides the development of water transport, Egremont was also responsible for road improvements. In 1784 the minute book of the Petworth Turnpike Trustees records a vote of thanks for 'his repeated acts of liberality towards the roads'.[41] In 1798 he prompted the re-routing of the turnpike past Coultershaw Mill instead of by Rotherbridge (see page 72). In 1803 he built the lane from Byworth to Lowheath and supported the Horsham Turnpike Act, 1811, which was opened from Five Oaks to Broadbridge Heath in 1813.

The Times obituary said: ' . . . he was not eminent as a statesman or warrior; neither illustrious for eloquence or genius; he was remarkable for one quality alone, and that was his immense benevolence'. To do good seemed to be his great characteristic and it is readily understandable that biographers have echoed in various terms Arthur Young's adulation when he wrote:

> It is impossible not to feel great respect, in contemplating the energy of an individual of the highest rank and fortune, animated with such ideas, and expending his income in so meritorious a manner, forming navigations, rewarding industry in the lower classes, improving the breed of livestock by bounties, encouraging all useful and mechanical artisans; setting on foot multiplied experiments to ascertain the comparative merit of different agricultural implements; introducing improvements, by extending the knowledge of new plants, animals, or implements, all of them in so many and various shapes contributing their assistance to national prosperity. The thought of one man having been instrumental in the improvement of his country, and still exerting himself in the same career, must be a constant fund of gratification to every benevolent mind; and that long may he live to enjoy the fruits of his labour in the service of his country, is the wish of every man in the county.[42]

CHAPTER THREE

CHOOSING A CONTRACTOR (1791)

William Jessop prepares the specification – tenders invited – Pinkerton's error – George Pinkerton's apology – contract awarded to Charles and Samuel Jones – Charles Jones, an unfortunate choice.

By the time Lord Egremont had obtained his Act of Parliament, the boom in canal building was underway.★ Thirty years had passed since the successful opening of the Bridgewater Canal and waterways were being started the length and breadth of Britain. Navigators to do the digging were becoming scarce. Only the previous October (1790) William Jessop had written to Lord Sheffield, at Sheffield Park, regarding the Upper Ouse Navigation† and had remarked that there were 'so many works of this kind in hand and so many more likely to come forward next season that workmen will be very scarce, especially artificers'.[43]

Jessop proposed to build the Rother Navigation by using the natural course of the river as far as possible. In April 1791 he wrote from Newark setting out the specifications which included the need for six passing places every mile, none to be more than 350 yards from the next. Nine locks were planned – later reduced to eight by increasing the rise of each lock by 6 inches – and some fifteen cuts made to avoid the worst sinuosities of the river and artificial obstructions like the water mills at Fittleworth and Lodsbridge. In this manner the natural length of the river between Midhurst and Stopham was to be reduced by 2 miles to 11½ miles. The longest cut was to be that leading from the Arun 600 yards west of where that river received the Rother. This 1,170 yard cutting traversed the grounds of Stopham House and was to be crossed by a stone occupational bridge leading to South Barn Farm. This proposal would not normally be one to appeal to a landowner, whose family had

---

★   The canal mania was in many respects a counterpart to the railway boom of 1845. Between 1792 and 1794, Acts were passed for over 1,000 miles of new inland navigation.

†   The Act of 1790 authorized the improvement of the Sussex Ouse from above Lewes to Upper Rylands Bridge. On 17 November 1790 Thomas, James and Francis Pinkerton undertook to build the navigation by 30 May 1792, but they had to abandon the contract in August 1792.

owned the estate for some seven hundred years and who had only recently rebuilt the family mansion within 200 yards of the proposed cut. However, it was pointed out that an artificial cut would reduce the flooding and the then owner and occupier Mr Smyth★ raised no objection to Jessop's plan.

The locks, all of which were to be built of ashlars from the local quarries, were to be sited at Stopham, Fittleworth, Shopham, Coultershaw, Ladymead, Lodsbridge, Moorland and Todham. The fall between the locks was to range from 6 to 7 ft and the total rise to Midhurst Wharf was 54 ft. Basins 132 ft x 66 ft to hold three barges were also planned by Jessop at Midhurst and Rotherbridge, but although begun the latter was never completed as the wharfs at Coultershaw served the same purpose.†

As mentioned in Chapter One Jessop had estimated the cost in March 1790 at over £10,000, but Lord Egremont decided to make various changes. Initially his lordship had wished to have the towing-path pass beneath all the bridges; however, after seeking Jessop's advice in September and being told that arches of 20 ft span would necessitate raising them higher than need be (the sole advantage was that about three minutes would be saved in the passing of a bridge),‡ he had decided that this could only be justified at Ambersham and Shopham and the new bridges at Moorland Farm and Midhurst. Various minor alterations had also been made to the line so that the local cost was expected to be less.

In May 1791 advertisements drafted by Jessop appeared in 'the public papers' inviting tenders for building the Rother Navigation according to his specifications. The Petworth Estate Office received three replies. The lowest figure, £7,148, was proffered by Charles Jones and his son Samuel, of Greywell. William Weston, a young man with experience of the Oxford Canal, who had just built the triple-arched stone bridge over the Trent at Gainsborough and who was later to become a well-known canal engineer in America, tendered £7,713. The Pinkertons, the best-known contractors in southern England, £7,937.

★ Walter Smyth (1751–1837) was a Barttelot who assumed the name of Smyth in compliance with the will of his great aunt Mary Hamilton Smyth. He inherited the Stopham Estates on the death of his father in 1764. His mother died when he was sixteen and in 1772 he married Philadelphia, the only daughter of the Revd John Wickens of Petworth and Tillington by whom he had ten children. In 1787 Smyth rebuilt Stopham House. The oldest parts, which enclosed a paved courtyard at the back of the present house, were pulled down and new rooms added. Smyth served for many years as an officer of the Sussex militia and was an active magistrate. (*SAC*, vol. XXVII, p. 46. The house was further remodelled in 1842 and 1865)

† The accounts for the period ending 24 December 1792 include an item 'cut to intended wharf at Rotherbridge and making a basin £20'.

‡ Jessop did point out that sometimes, however, a great saving would arise when the river was in flood since casting off the towline could entail some delay while the barge was tightly secured to the bank.

Lord Egremont and his steward, James Upton Tripp, examined each of these and, after seeking Jessop's opinion, Tripp wrote to the applicants to clarify various details. The problem was that there was a lack of exactness in the interpretation of Jessop's specification. As Weston stressed in his reply, 'the very great uncertainty of the business' made 'any valuation extremely imperfect'. Indeed the very real problem for the proprietors of any intended navigation was to find an experienced and reliable builder, whose competitively priced estimate made sufficient allowance for the vagaries of the English climate. Such men were few and far between.

The Pinkertons' estimate was criticized by Jessop, who added £803 for items which had been omitted. On 23 May George Pinkerton (nephew of John) wrote to Lord Egremont apologizing for the error. 'Mr Jessop said we must have made some mistake in the quantity of cubic yards in the hill by Mr Smith's (*sic*)★ – and on a re-examination we found it so. I am extremely sorry we made such a mistake as it may carry the appearance of imposition which is a thing I durst not attempt in reality as I consider Lord Sheffield's good opinion of more consequence to me than any advantage gained by such a proceeding.' The Pinkerton's revised estimate dated 8 August 1791 was £8,740.

There was little to choose between any of the three, but Weston was, thought Jessop, too inexperienced. Pinkertons were well established but had blundered in their original estimate and their revised one was more than 20 per cent higher than the lowest tender. Although Jessop had worked with them on numerous occasions and had recommended them in the past, he had found them no better than the general run of contractors.[44] In a letter to Lord Sheffield in September 1792, Jessop wrote that he was 'too well satisfied of the misconduct of the Pinkertons to need any further proof of it'. There seemed no good reason therefore not to accept the lowest tender and so the contract was awarded to the Jones's on 26 August 1791, the signing being witnessed by Tripp and Thomas Poling Upton.

The Jones's were unable to provide any surety other than their own, but Tripp suggested that this difficulty could be mitigated if it was agreed that the Jones's were to purchase timber from the estate at the same price as his lordship sold it to his timber merchant, which would save the contractor the cost of carriage; also it was proposed, and later agreed, that if Charles Jones was to act in any way contrary to the contract, 'it shall rest with the Earl of Egremont to dismiss him at Fittleworth, Shopham Bridge, Coultershaw Mill, Rotherbridge, etc.'.

★ In other words in the grounds of Stopham House, the residence of Mr Walter Smyth.

However, Jessop should have known, and most probably did, that there were good reasons for not awarding the contract to the Jones's. It is probable that he confided his doubts to both his lordship and to Tripp, but felt in the circumstances that Charles Jones was the best man available in spite of his shortcomings. Only two years before, when Jessop had been the consultant engineer on the Basingstoke Canal, Jones had been engaged in building Greywell Tunnel;* indeed he styled himself 'Architect of Greywell'. In August 1789 the main contractor, John Pinkerton, had, with his 'privity and consent', agreed to Jones's dismissal on the grounds of 'improper conduct', almost certainly drunkenness, and the proprietors had stipulated that he was never to be engaged again on any of the canal works.[45] Yet what gives food for thought is that a fortnight later Pinkerton requested the management committee to reinstate him. The proprietors would not hear of it – Jones had certainly offended members of the management committee, not only at the time of their recent survey, 'but previous to it' – and in November they moved a resolution that the meeting do particularly request that the committee should 'continue to interfere in all such cases'.[46]

Nor was that all. Charles Jones had a past of which Jessop was seemingly ignorant. It appears that in the 1770s Jones had worked in the Manchester area as a mason and as a miner; moving from job to job, he had left debts unpaid and gained a reputation for singular ineptitude, if not downright dishonesty. However, in 1783 he had successfully tendered for driving the 2-mile long Sapperton Tunnel on the Thames & Severn Canal on the recommendation of Josiah Clowes, the resident engineer, as one 'well qualified by Experience to take the Conduct & Management' of the work. The Thames & Severn management committee knew little of his character, but it was not long before they discovered that Jones failed to pay his men regularly and that he was unreliable. However, by the time the committee learnt that his two sureties were not forthcoming, he had already been at work several months. Although he was arrested three times for debt and sent to gaol, he managed to avoid breaking his agreement with the company, who could dismiss him if he was absent for twenty-eight days at any time. The part of the tunnel which Jones was building made little progress; after a portion of the roof had collapsed and he had gone off on a lengthy drinking spree, he was given three months' notice to complete the work he had begun and then to quit. Jones, feeling aggrieved, did little more and retaliated with the threat of legal proceedings; some years later (in 1792) he unsuccessfully filed a bill in

---

* At least one of the Rother Navigation workmen, Benjamin Baigent, had also been employed at Greywell.

Chancery actually claiming that he had built the tunnel.[47] The Thames & Severn proprietors, when defending the action, stated that Jones owed the company over £1,900 and recorded that they had 'found him neither a skilful artist, attentive to his business nor honorable, but vain, shifty and artfull in all his dealings'.[48]

This then was the character who had undertaken to complete the navigation to Rotherbridge by 1 January 1793 and to Midhurst by 1 January 1794. No tunnels, however, were needed for the Rother Navigation (Hardham Canal Tunnel, which joined the Rivers Arun and Rother, was part of the Arun Navigation which had been opened in 1789), and the work expected of the Jones's was by the standards of the day quite straightforward. The chief hazard was likely to be floods damaging the works, occurrences which the neighbouring Arun Canal regularly suffered.

The relationship between the consultant engineer and the contractor was always liable to difficulty, especially if the former was often absent and the latter inexperienced, unreliable or simply incompetent. Before work commenced Jessop set out the line of the waterway, indicated the location of the bridges, locks, weirs and culverts and formed a general opinion of the amount of excavating, levelling and embanking. Then he drew the plans, sketched the design for the bridges, wrote the directions for the execution of the locks and the artificial cuts. His advice was sought on the best places to site weirs so that the overflow did not damage the banks, to which he replied: 'The floodgates that are used at the several mills are proper patterns to make others by.'

It was the Jones's responsibility to hire the labour and to carry out the digging and the building of the various engineering works; in particular to ensure that the locks and their various components were set out accurately and made to the proper dimensions, and that the materials were good and well put together. Jessop could only hope that Samuel Jones would keep his father up to the mark.

CHAPTER FOUR

THE BUILDING OF THE ROTHER NAVIGATION (1791–5)

Cutting begun in August 1791 – stone quarries opened up – Rother Navigation completed to Fittleworth (1792) and Coultershaw (1793) – Gilbert White's meteorological observations – failure of the contractors (1793) – Lord Egremont employs his own men – Arthur Young comments on the advantages – appearance and dress of two navigators – first tolls collected – death of Viscount Montague and the burning of Cowdray House (1793) – first barge to reach Midhurst (1794) – completion of the basin (1795) – celebratory feast, June 1795.

The chill of autumn was already in the air when in late August 1791 the first turf was cut from the grounds of Stopham House. There was 'a fair amount' of excavating to be accomplished as 20 ft and more of sand and clay had to be removed from the cutting through the hillock in the park. Never before had Stopham seen so much bustle and commotion. A visitor would have seen a hundred men at work digging out 'High Field', wheeling away the excavated soil to fill in the large swamp and hollows north of the lock site. All around were 'navigation' barrows and hand-barrows, a pile engine, scoops, buckets, 'tarrace'* beaters, 'tarrace' tubs, axes, beetles (used for flattening the earth banks), grafting tools, mattocks, picks and saws. By the carpenter's large tool chest, strapped with iron bands, stood a grindstone, and not far away a huge iron kettle was kept heated for the hot water needed throughout the day.

Once the digging had been completed the 'great ballast barge' came up from Arundel laden with planks of memel timber, while the 'lesser barge' brought brick clay from the local pits. Throughout that winter the navigators toiled and pushed as barrowload after barrowload of earth was deposited and spread on either side of the deep trench rapidly taking shape.

When the contractor brought his men to Stopham in 1791 to begin work on the Rother Navigation they found themselves among countrymen dependent on agricultural work for their livelihood. Canal building in

---

* Tarras, a kind of rock similar to pozzolana, imported from Holland for making mortar.

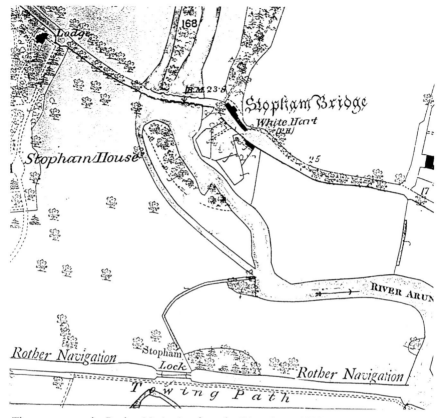

The entrance to the Rother Navigation from the River Arun, 1876.

southern England was in its infancy and Lord Egremont's craftsmen were soon needed to assist the Jones's in their task. Often enough their work necessitated contingency assistance. Floods, ice and snow created unexpected difficulties which often threatened to, and did, bring work to a standstill. Ploughmen helped to shift wagon-loads of spoil and sand from meadow or quarry. Local masons, carpenters, wheelwrights and ironsmiths were called upon to build the lock chambers, gates and paddles and to fit the ironwork. Together they formed a motley group of men who required constant encouragement to overcome the elements. Most Saturday nights they filled the White Hart (the alehouse by Stopham Bridge) drinking, singing and expressing their good fortune in being actively employed. However, their daily wage of 1s 4d was a little below the average for a farm labourer, who could generally expect 1s 6d

The White Hart by Stopham Bridge, 1952. The bridge was built during the reign of
Edward III. In the seventeenth century a drawbridge facilitated the passage of boats. In 1822
the central arch was raised to allow more heavily laden barges to pass.

in West Sussex in the 1790s.[49] Doubtless, however, they had heard rumours of
what was happening only 30 miles away on the Ouse Navigation, where
progress was very slow and Lord Sheffield was complaining to Jessop in
December about how Pinkertons had fallen behind with the work. Jessop
sagely replied that 'even under the best management I always find that in the
progress of execution, there are such a variety of unforeseen disappointments,
so many delays arising from the negligence of workmen of all descriptions . . .
and so many knaves among them . . . I can foresee that the impression will
wear off when you have put them into a better train of proceeding'.[50]

Jessop, however, had less and less time to spare to visit the works on the
Rother. In a letter to James Upton from London, dated 4 April 1792, he
writes: 'I have not yet been able to go down to you and I cannot for some
time hence.' Instead he contented himself with giving advice whenever asked.
The Jones's asked numerous questions such as how best to mix the 'terras'
with mortar, how to prevent silting at the tail of a cut and how many conduits
there should be for filling each lock.[51]

Some of the problems facing the contractors at work in the Rother Valley

A line of poplars indicates the entrance to the Rother Navigation at Stopham, 1952.

can be judged from Gilbert White's contemporary observations at nearby Selborne.[52] The daily rainfall measurements and annual weather summaries, which White had begun in 1768, provide a fairly accurate picture of the conditions which the 'navigators' had to face only a dozen or so miles to the south-east.

The splendid start occasioned by the fine harvest weather in August and September 1791 had given way to a wet October and an even wetter and stormier November, when over 8 inches of rain were recorded at Selborne, the heaviest monthly fall for over a decade. It was a contractor's nightmare. The meadows bordering the river were in many places underwater; planks and fence posts were washed away; the canal cuts beginning to take shape were soon turned into ponds into which the heavy rains washed back the newly excavated spoil piled high along the banks. There was much frost in December which continued until February 1792; March was wet and cold. William Lucas spent five days pitching wattles in Mr Smyth's field.

The arrival of spring brought a welcome change. Except for a great storm on 13 April, a spell of very warm weather enabled good progress on the

Stopham Lock, 1987.

navigation to be made. May and June continued cold and dry. Although July was wet and cool, the excavations had been completed to Coultershaw Wharf by the end of the month. In August John Hartwell received 4s for taking out a miry place, putting in bavins and mending the new road at Stopham Meadows.

Some fifty to sixty men were employed. The chief carpenters Charles Bridger and Robert Russel had to ensure the exact measurement of all the woodwork, which was essential if the lock-gates were to be correctly balanced. John Lincott was the sawyer; Henry Hersee did the iron work; Herbert Parker mixed the mortar. Thomas Mills was the overseer 'to see that the works were done in a workmanlike manner'. He received 2s 6d a day while the navigators were paid 1s 4d. September 1792 was a busy month, with activity all along the line between Stopham and Ladymead locks, and extra payments made to men working the harvest. Samuel Andrews was barging stone from Coombelands and lime from Pulborough to Stopham. Messrs Digance were bringing up coal from Arundel for the brickyard

Swan Bridge, Pulborough, 1891. At centre left was the entrance to the cut which allowed barges to unload grain for the corn exchange and there was also a dock on the left bank just above the bridge. In the 1830s the Arundel Lighter Company's boats passed by daily to convey goods to London, Chichester and Portsmouth (Pigot's Sussex Directory, 1832).

worked by Stephen Russel at Fittleworth, where 18,000 bricks were moulded that month. The problems at the brickyard had been resolved by John Horner from Bognor, who had come over twice to see to the brick burner and to 'direct about the bricks'. The stone pits which had been opened all around were working at full capacity. At Rotherbridge Hanger stone blocks were being quarried for Coultershaw Lock; at Bridewell Pit, Petworth, for Shopham Lock; at Lodsworth for Ladymead Lock. Different types of stone came from different pits. Coping was taken from Upperton Common, scapel from Pitshill, rough from Lisagate Common and ashlar from Vinen Lane, North Heath, where the men spent six and a half days 'trying for stone'. Moving stone was slow and difficult work; it took nine days for Henry Saigeman to barge 64 tons from Mr Blunden's pit to Stopham Lock.

The first reference to the navigation being used occurs on 29 September: 'One shilling paid for getting boat to water'. On 13 October Samuel Andrews was paid £1 11s 6d for barging stone to Stopham Lock and a separate entry on the same day refers to three barge-loads of stone from the lock to the

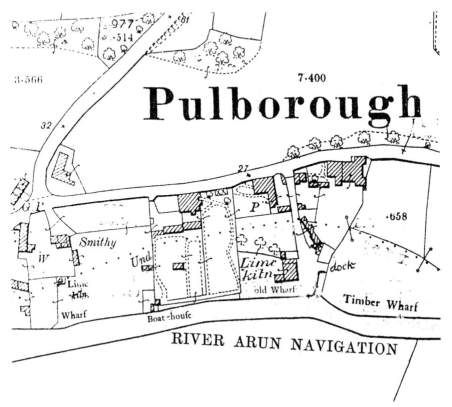

The river bank at Pulborough in 1876. The straightening of the River Arun during the second half of the sixteenth century caused wharves to be established along the north bank and lime-kilns to be built. The dotted line on the map indicates the former course of the river before it was diverted. The dock by the lime-kiln depicted on the 1851 tithe map was last used in the 1870s.

tumble bay. Stopham Lock was completed and on 10 November 1792 Lord Egremont paid £8 17s 6d for 'a feast to the navigators at Fittleworth' to celebrate the completion of the first part of the navigation.

The Jones's had been confident that they would reach Rotherbridge by the end of the year, but it was not to be. The year 1792 had proved a wretched one weatherwise. The harvest was late and wet and in spite of one or two fine spells in November, most days proved wet and windy. The Midhurst area had the highest annual rainfall for twelve years and much time and expense was incurred in bringing back the workmen's paraphernalia, timber and wattles,

The substantial late seventeenth- or early eighteenth-century lime-kiln on the Old Wharf at Pulborough as seen in the 1930s. The stone lime-kiln had two furnaces and measured 40 ft × 30 ft. On the east side was the dock which silted up in the 1870s (it is not marked on the 1876 survey). A few posts and piles remained in 1953. In June 1789 the Arun Navigation Company leased the Old Wharf from the devisees of Thomas Hampton for ninety-nine years at £6 per year and in December 1804 the company agreed that Thomas Stone should maintain the wharf for the benefit of the bargemen.

which were carried away by what Upton termed 'very great floods'. Thomas Lucas spent five days 'getting plank back that was drove away by the flood'.

In December Upton paid £1 3s 6d for 'gin and beer for Mr Jones's men working in the water bottoming the wharf at Shopham Bridge'. Three weeks later, against a similar entry of £2 6s 0d, is written: 'because it was so far to go and many times they were forced to work in the water'.

It was not only the weather which turned against the contractors, but the lack of skilled workmen who had drifted away to seek jobs advertised elsewhere. Similar difficulties were facing canal contractors in other parts of the country. In East Sussex the Pinkertons were forced to abandon the Ouse contract in August 1792. Jessop, asked by Lord Sheffield to nominate an engineer to take charge of the remaining construction, could only reply that so numerous were the works now in hand that he knew of no one disengaged

The author examining nature's efforts to reclaim the walls of Stopham Lock and the site of the upper gates, 1987.

whom he could recommend, and doubtless reflected that only five days earlier he had reported to the directors of the Leicester Navigation (where he was the principal engineer) that the Pinkertons (James, George and Francis) were not executing the works on the navigation to his satisfaction. To Lord Sheffield Jessop added that

> if you would give me the navigation, I could not at present find a man that would suit you. In two or three works in which I am concerned* they are

---

* Jessop was at this time chief engineer of the Cromford Canal (1789–94), the Nottingham Canal (1790–6) and the Leicester Navigation (1791–5). The first and last of these companies paid Jessop £350 p.a. on the understanding that he gave one third of his time to the job. In 1792 he was acting as consulting engineer on the Sussex Ouse and Rother Navigations, while also engaged in building two major aqueducts over the Amber and Derwent rivers so it is not surprising that after taking into account the time he had to spend in London on parliamentary work (appearing before three House of Lords committees in 1792) he was grossly overworking.

The stone occupation bridge over the navigation in the grounds of Stopham House, 1889.

nearly at a standstill for want of all descriptions of workmen – and I cannot conceive how the Numerous Schemes now in agitation can be executed in less than double the time that was formerly necessary. For my own part I am harassed beyond endurance and hate the sight of the Post that brings me Letters.[53]

Canal mania was at its height. On 18 August the *London Gazette* contained no less than nineteen notices of intended applications to Parliament for leave to make canals in different parts of the kingdom.

The Jones's struggled on during the spring of 1793, employing various subcontractors, but in spite of relatively dry weather, by June they were forced to face the realities of the situation and had to withdraw from the contract.★

It seems very probable that Charles Jones left the Rother at Jessop's

★ The contract was finally rescinded on 29 November 1793. The accounts show that the Jones's had received £1,536 11*s* 9*d* more than they were due, which as they were unable to repay, Lord Egremont had agreed to waive the debt on condition that all the materials and utensils along the works, valued at £713 19*s* 11*d* and purchased by himself, should become his sole property. (PHA F13/9/19)

Moorland Bridge crossed the navigation cut between South Ambersham and Selham. Note the tow-path beneath the arch.

instigation to work on the Grand Junction Canal. On 5 June 1793 Jessop had been appointed its chief engineer. Within days a contract 'prepared under the direction of Mr Jessop' had been awarded to Charles Jones and John Biggs to build Braunston Tunnel, and two more contracts were signed in December for Blisworth and Langleybury tunnels.[54] One can only conclude that tunnellers were in such short supply that Jessop had no other alternative but to accept a contractor whose record at Sapperton and Greywell was so undistinguished. When Jessop came to report on their progress in May 1794, 'he wished the contractors at Braunston would get on with the work with more vigour'. At Blisworth he considered that Jones had rushed into the job without making proper preparations. Some of the brickwork was so poor it needed replacing, his brickyards were behind hand and he had no equipment ready for raising spoil from the pits. Jessop went on, 'he is much wanting in management and economy. I wish he may not be found to be incorrigible.'[55] It was not long before both contractors had run into difficulties and in September they gave up the contract.

The contractors' failure at Petworth was inconvenient but not serious. In July Lord Egremont paid 10*s* 7*d* for two advertisements in the Reading paper for men to work on the navigation. The notice which appeared in the *Reading Mercury* on 29 July and 5 August 1793 read, 'WANTED immediately, from 50 to 100 CUTTERS. They will meet with the best prices given, by applying to Mr Samuel Jones, contractor of the above navigation, Petworth, Sussex. Likewise several BRICKLAYERS, STONE-MASONS, and CARPENTERS wanted who will meet with good encouragement, by applying as above'.

Lord Egremont, receiving little or no response to these advertisements, decided to adopt the obvious solution of employing his own men under the supervision of Thomas Upton.* As Arthur Young junior wrote, this had its own particular advantages:

> In the usual method of cutting canals, these men are a constant nuisance to the neighbourhood, and the terror of all other descriptions of people. But in Lord Egremont's canal, the men are all drawn from amongst his own workmen, and have none of that turbulence and riot with which foreign workmen are inspired; and as these labourers use implements equal to the best navigation diggers, the employment of domestic workmen is an evident advantage; and still farther, the expenses of the job are much less to the employer, whilst the weekly wages of the men in this business, instead of 8*s* or 9*s* rise up to 14*s* or 15*s*.†

The normal practice was for contractors to employ professional labourers who travelled round the country from canal to canal. These navigators, or 'navvies' as they were called, were accustomed to the work and therefore generally more efficient than casual labour. However, they were distrusted by the local populace for a variety of reasons, not least because of their thieving ways (particularly poaching) and bouts of drunkenness. The Duke of Bridgewater had used men from his estate to dig his canal, but efforts by companies to provide local employment were not always successful. Soon after the building of the Basingstoke Canal had begun in the autumn of 1788, the Revd Stebbing Shaw, viewing a hundred or so men at work preparing the approach to Greywell Tunnel, commented that

---

* Thomas Upton appears to have taken over in August 1793 for his first accounts, dated 24th, are for labour engaged on works begun by Mr Jones below Lodsbridge.

† Upton's accounts show that the navigators were paid 1*s* 4*d* a day. Craftsmen such as carpenters and masons received 2*s* and the gang supervisor 2*s* 6*d*.

the contractor, agreeable to the request of the company of proprietors, gives the preference to all the natives desirous of this work, but such is the power of use over nature, that while these industrious poor are by all their efforts incapable of earning a sustenance, those who are brought from similar works, cheerfully obtain a comfortable support.[56]

Among the payments made during 1794 were ¾ day spent at Sutton Meadow sifting seeds in Mr Hurst's hayloft, paying James Hurst for sewing the banks with hayseed, tipping the foreman at Iping Paper Mill to hold back the water, giving the miller at Stedham 2s for drink. In April Steer & Co. provided the gunpowder and my lord the tools, for blowing and breaking 28 loads of stone.

Some impression of the type of men who built the Rother Navigation can be gained from the circulated descriptions of two labourers wanted for sheep stealing in April 1796.[57]

William Lucas was about thirty years old and had lived almost all his life at Petworth. He was 5 ft 7 in tall, 'thin and straight made – of a dark brown hair'. He had the habit of 'chewing tobacco very much' and while working on the navigation between October 1792 and January 1795 his fellow navvies called him 'Bean-Liquor'. His dress when last seen was 'a short coarse wrapper round frock, a striped jacket, an under flannel waist-coat, coarse linen breeches and long black military spadderdashes'.

Benjamin Baigent was known as 'Big Ben'. Aged about thirty-six he was 6 ft tall, raw-boned, strongly made but not very stout, of a dark brown complexion, with a stiff, sawing gait and rather curly brown hair. He also chewed tobacco. He had previously worked for '3 or 4 years' at Greywell Tunnel on the Basingstoke Canal, but 'lately about Petworth on the Rother Navigation and is suspected to have gone from there to the Newbury Navigation'.* When he departed he was wearing 'a stout Russia round frock, a white flannel jacket and long Russia trousers'. Upton's accounts show that Baigent worked regularly on the navigation between December 1793 and May 1795; in the latter month he was digging out the foundations for a sluice on the Petworth Canal. He was also employed at the pond in Petworth Park after the navigation was completed.

The evidence given at the Sussex Assizes reveals a dismal picture of peasant life at the time the navigation was built. Sheep stealing was a capital offence (until 1832), and even until 1853 convictions could carry the penalty of

---

* Work had begun at Newbury on the Kennet & Avon Canal in June 1794. The 6 mile section to Kintbury was opened in June 1797.

transportation for life. Circumstantial evidence in this case, if it could be believed, told heavily against Rowland Harper, the only one of the three accused who had been apprehended and who had been advised to make a confession.

The first witness, Joseph Legg, stated that Harper and William Lucas had asked him to join them one Saturday night to get some mutton. He had declined. The next morning he had found half a dead sheep in the cellar of the house where he and Harper resided. Another witness, Jane Slater, who had been a lodger with the Harper family in Byworth, said that for the first six weeks of her stay the family had lived very poorly on 'turnip greens and other vegetables, and with scarcely any meat'; however, after the sheep was stolen, 'mutton seemed very plenty . . . sometimes boiled, but oftener fried or put into puddings'. A third witness, Lydia Lee, who resided near Harper in Byworth Street, said that she frequently bought hog-wash (pigswill) from the prisoner, and about a week after the sheep was stolen she found pieces of mutton suet in the wash and the tail-gut which, when squeezed, exuded very fresh sheep's dung; about that time she also frequently saw the prisoner's children eating dressed mutton. Then Harper's mother claimed she had bought mutton for 21d at Petworth market on a Saturday, but could not remember exactly which Saturday, while Stephen Elliott stated he had sold her no meat since her husband died. The assize judge was disinclined to accept the confession or the circumstantial evidence, probably because two of the miscreants could not be found, and Harper was acquitted.

The collection of tolls began on the Rother Navigation in late May or early June 1793. A surviving record[58] shows that toll ticket no. 43 was issued at Fittleworth on 5 August to bargemaster Samuel Andrews for 15 tons of tub staves from Coultershaw Wharf to the Arun.

In November Lord Egremont held a feast for 'the work people' to celebrate the opening of the navigation to Coultershaw for which Jonathan Johnson received the not inconsiderable sum of £36 5s 8d. Other disbursements included two guineas for ribbons.

The wretchedness of these men working in all weathers, often knee-deep in mud, was little relieved when they returned home to their cottages whose floors, whether of earth, stone or brick and seldom covered with more than straw or sacking, were invariably extremely damp during the winter months. Their miserly diet, illustrated by the evidence in the Harper sheep stealing case, added nothing to their happiness. The excitement of a feast day can therefore be well imagined. By the end of the year 160 barges had passed through Fittleworth Lock carrying some 2,800 tons.

Meantime there had been a double tragedy. On the night of 24 September Cowdray House had been destroyed by fire, and in October its owner, the

The ruins of Cowdray House viewed from the River Rother. The bridge is situated above the site of the former wharf. The house was destroyed by fire in 1793.

24-year-old Viscount Montague, had been drowned on the Rhine when he might have been boating on the Rother.★ The only references to his lordship's interest in the navigation occur in the Act of Parliament and in the payment to him on 14 December 1793 of £21 6s 2d for timber and faggots.

The weather still posed serious problems during 1794. However, in March there is a reference to a boat or small barge travelling from Lodsbridge to Midhurst; in April 2s 6d was paid for fetching back the pump 'drove away' by the flood; in May Charles Bridger, the chief carpenter, spent four days cutting

---

★   Montague was travelling with a friend on the Continent, when on arriving at Schaffhausen they rashly decided to shoot the falls in a flat-bottomed boat. After successfully passing the first group of rocks, eyewitnesses reported that they began to shout and wave their handkerchiefs in token of success. They then pushed down the second falls, by far more dangerous than the first, after which they were seen or heard no more. Presumably the boat overturned and they were carried away by the volume of the cataract and sucked down by the vortex. The property was inherited by Lord Montague's sister Elizabeth Mary Browne (1767–1830), who married William Poyntz (1770–1840) in 1794. Although they resided in the converted keeper's lodge for the rest of their lives and made no attempt to rebuild the house they placed the estate on a sound footing. Since both Poyntz's sons were drowned in a boating mishap at Bognor in 1815, the Cowdray estate passed to his three daughters. As difficulties arose about dividing the property, it was sold in 1843 to the 6th Earl of Egmont.

down the lock-gates at Stopham to let the floods through. That same month James Stoveld received 16s 6d for repairing the long screw pump.

In July Lodsbridge Wharf was in use and Ambersham Bridge pulled down and rebuilt with the tow-path beneath. In August bricks were being barged from Pallingham; the partially finished bridge at Moorland was causing problems to the horses drawing the hay wagons, a difficulty overcome by giving the carters 2s 'for drink'. More serious was the damage caused at Fittleworth by Mr Satter's hogs getting into William Chalk's garden through the navigation fence; compensation of 10s had to be paid. In September the lock-gates were hung at Todham and a thousand bricks were boated down from Midhurst; a drain 110 yards long was also cut through the basin at Midhurst to take the brook under the new bridge from South Pond.

In October Robert Russel received 3s 6d for drink for finishing his last lock, and in November the first barge reached Midhurst carrying stone from the quarry at Spershots Hanger, near Rotherbridge, with which to build the bridge across the entrance to the basin. Meanwhile William Jessop wrote to Lord Egremont from Newark advising him about William Dale's* claim for compensation for loss of water power at Coultershaw.[59] In the letter Jessop states that Dale is quite mistaken and that 'he has lately forgot to mention the only circumstances on which with any shew of reason he could ground a complaint', and goes on to point out that the only real injury is the loss of a lock-full of water, worth about 3d, when he is grinding corn.

Early in December disaster struck. 'A very great flood' swamped the excavations at Midhurst and swept away a small bridge at Todham, where so great was the devastation to the banks that William White, working the ballast barge, had to have a team of twenty men making good. Over 2,000 tons of sand had to be barged down from Midhurst Steep Hanger to repair the damage. The weather had now turned very cold. In December ten bottles of gin and much beer were required for the men before they would get into the water in the mornings to bottom the basin.

The first barge loaded with coal reached Midhurst on New Year's Eve 1794. William Day and Edward Mills had spent two and a half days assisting the barge up and helping to unload her, 'as there was a very hard frost and it was very difficult getting through the ice in the new cut and the landing place was not made'.† In February one shilling had to be spent on 'sticking up

---

* Young records that the miller had fattened a hog which weighed 728 lb, its 'pisser' 2 lb.

† According to Professor Manley's Central England Temperature Series, January 1795 was the coldest month ever, with a mean daily temperature of less than 27 degrees Fahrenheit.

The canal basin and wharfingers' cottage at Midhurst, 1898. The wharf ceased to be used for pleasure boating in 1912.

notices concerning damage wantonly done to the navigation'. On Ash Wednesday Lord Egremont ordered that the forty-six navvies and the boy James Hill should be paid sums varying from 1*s* to 3*s* 'for Fast Day'. Continuous wet weather hampered work to complete the basin, which was being built large enough (132 ft x 66 ft) to receive three barges. A newly built quay collapsed and had to be repiled. Not until April were the basin and the 150-yd-long road leading to the turnpike completed. Lastly, fences had to be erected and coal pens laid out.

Lord Egremont celebrated the completion of the navigation by arranging a grand feast at Midhurst. On Wednesday 24 June 1795 a gaily decorated barge brought guests, refreshed with generous draughts of beer,★ from Rotherbridge to the new basin. James Champion provided a variety of good fare at a cost of £42 and the events of the day were highlighted by firing the cannon for which Samuel Andrews had provided the gunpowder (value 18*s*.).

★ 'Paid for beer had by people at Rotherbridge going to the Feast at Midhurst, 24 June 1795, 18 shillings'. (PHA 2931)

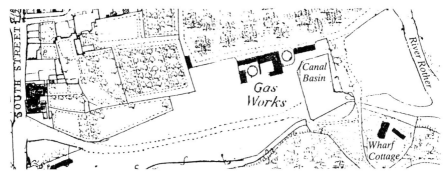

The canal basin at Midhurst (1874) marked the terminus of the navigation. The bridge over the entrance to the wharf and the cottage still stand.

It must have been a scene of great rejoicing and it is easy to imagine the hubbub as some two hundred men, women and children ate, drank, sang and danced around the wharf, which had been festooned with flags and bunting for the occasion. There is no record of those who actually attended this jolly function nor of what transpired, but it can safely be assumed that Lord Egremont and the leading dignitaries of Petworth and Midhurst congratulated Upton and his men on a job well done which could but reduce the price of coal and bring prosperity to his lordship and to the inhabitants of the Rother Valley.

CHAPTER FIVE

THE ARUN NAVIGATION'S DILEMMA
(1791–6)

The Arun Navigation Company's financial difficulties – relationship between the proprietors and Lord Egremont – the Arun's petition to extend their navigation to Kirdford and to above Stopham Lock (1792) – reasons for Lord Egremont's opposition – failure of petition – extension proposed to Horsham (1793) – Sir Harry Goring resigns as Chairman and Lord Egremont becomes a major shareholder in the Arun Navigation Company (1796).

By 1791 water communication was open from the sea to Arundel for vessels up to 200 tons and for barges as far as Newbridge. However, the river between Arundel and Pallingham, a distance of 18¼ miles, remained a public navigation free of toll. There was no tow-path; barges either sailed or were punted up and down the river with the tide. The journey from Littlehampton to Newbridge took about two and a half days, although six hours were saved if Hardham Tunnel was used. Most of the barges were spritsailed and could carry in excess of 30 tons, although the loads were related more to draught than to capacity, being dependent on the rains rather than the tides on the upper reaches of the river.

The passing of the Rother Navigation Act brought little satisfaction to the proprietors of the Arun Navigation Company. Although they anticipated that some revenue would accrue from Rother barges using the Coldwaltham Cut, it would not be sufficient to defray the expense of the Arun's statutory duty to maintain the tideway between Houghton and Pallingham. Young later confirmed their fears when he reported that the tolls for this new cut drove much trade to the old river channel 'except in summer or in floods'.[60]

Not surprisingly the Arun proprietors made no effort to maintain the river above Greatham and it was this failure that prompted the merchants, tradesmen and inhabitants of Pulborough to petition the House of Commons in 1791 to acquaint the

Honourable House that the river is now in a worse state for the purpose of navigation than at the time the Act was obtained (1785) and unless

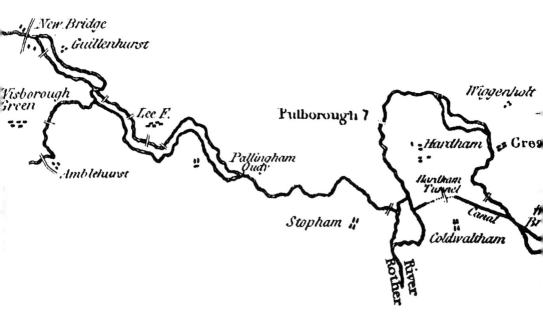

Plan of the navigation of the River Arun from the sea to Newbridge, 1790.

provision be made for the speedy and effectual carrying into execution the purposes intended by the said Act, so far as relates to the amending and improving the navigation of the river, your petitioners and many other persons residing or having estates within the said town must be very great sufferers and their trade materially injured if not entirely lost.

It was this fact that had persuaded Lord Egremont to consider initially including the River Arun between Greatham and Stopham in his bill for the Rother Navigation and the reason for Jessop's survey in 1789.

Until the opening of the Wey & Arun Junction Canal in 1816, all, or nearly all, of the Rother's traffic originated from, or was destined to, the Arun Navigation. Thus the Rother's dependence on the smooth running of the Arun was as much its concern as it was that of the Arun proprietors who one would have hoped would have been in agreement with the plans and projects of Lord Egremont. Unfortunately this was not the case.

In the first place the fifteen or so proprietors of the Arun were primarily local merchants and farmers investing in what they hoped would become a

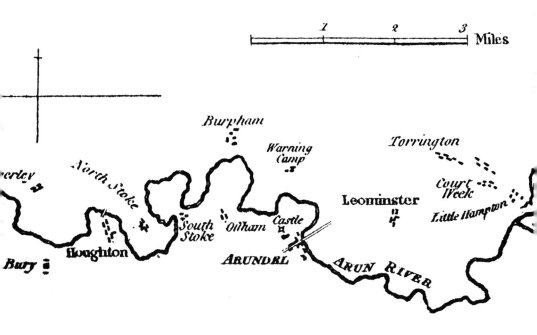

prosperous enterprise, whereas the earl was more concerned with the improvement of his Petworth Estate. Secondly, the proprietors of the Arun were in serious financial difficulty since the cost of building the navigation had exceeded the estimate by some 60 per cent. Only £7,000 of the authorized share capital of £10,000 had been raised and some £9,000 had had to be borrowed on mortgage of the tolls to complete the navigation. Thirdly, the estimated carriage of 30,000 tons a year had yet to materialize. Traffic during the first twelve months of full operation only amounted to 14,000 tons, which yielded an annual income barely sufficient to meet the running expenses and pay the interest on the mortgage.

The correspondence concerning the Arun Navigation Company's proposals to further extend their navigation indicates that the relationship between the company and Lord Egremont was not of the best. It was aggravated also by the fact that whereas the Arun proprietors were legally bound to maintain the tidal reaches of the river above Houghton, they were not empowered to charge tolls on river traffic.

Early in 1792 concern was expressed by Lord Egremont's advisers at talk of

No Tolls to be taken upon the Old River *Arun*, from *Great-ham Bridge* to *Stopham Bridge*.

XVI. Provided also, and it is hereby further enacted, That no Toll shall be paid for the Passage of any Boat, Barge, or Lighter whatsoever, whether loaded or unloaded, or for any Goods, Wares, or Merchandizes whatsoever, that shall be carried and conveyed on the old Stream called the River Arun, to Pulborough, Stopham, or Pallenham, unless such Boat, Barge, Lighter, or other Vessel, shall go through the intended new Cut from Greatham Bridge to Stopham Bridge, and pass the Lock to be erected and set up in such new Cut, so that the Navigation of that Part of the old River Arun, from Greatham Bridge to Stopham Bridge, shall not be impeded or obstructed by any Locks, Bays, Dams, Piles, or other Obstacles or Obstructions whatsoever, but shall be and remain free and open for the Passage of Boats, Barges, Lighters, and other Vessels, without being subject to any Tolls or Duties whatsoever, any Thing in this present Act contained to the contrary in anywise notwithstanding.

The controversial Section XVI of the Act of Parliament, 1785, which ensured that the Arun Navigation Company could not change tolls for the use of the river up to Pallingham although the company shall 'make and maintain an effectual and proper navigation for vessels drawing 3' 1" of water'.

the Arun proprietors petitioning Parliament for a further Act. At their meeting the previous December the proprietors had in fact agreed to apply for a bill to build a branch canal from above Orfold Lock (the top lock on the Arun Canal) to Fisher Street, North Chapel by Wisborough Green, Kirdford and Shillinglee Lake.★

Henry Tripp,† Lord Egremont's London attorney, wrote from Stone

---

★ The purpose of the scheme was stated as 'public utility and improvement of land and estates', but more important must have been the fact that both Kirdford and North Chapel furnished substantial deposits of Petworth marble.

† The fifth and youngest son of John Tripp, Deputy Recorder of Taunton. Henry was a barrister of Lincoln's Inn and agent for Egremont's West of England estates for over fifty years. He died in 1835.

Horses towing barges had to cross the River Arun at Stopham by this wooden 'gallows' bridge – a flat beam high above the water with an inclined plane on each side. This 1889 view shows Hardham Mill in the background. A red iron bridge replaced the wooden bridge in about 1914.

Buildings in the Temple to his brother James Upton Tripp, who was the Sussex agent, on 31 January 1792 to say that he would try and obtain any facts or knowledge of the intentions of the Arun proprietors, stating that 'it will be impossible for me to be of any use before the (parliamentary) committee if I am not furnished with instructions and those instructions supported by evidence', and urging that 'it is absolutely necessary that you should be here to see the Plan and the Bill'. Tripp advised his lordship to collect as many friends as he could to oppose the petition before the committee, but the following day he reported that the Arun proprietors had not yet moved. In fact they waited until 28 February when their clerk, William Carleton, wrote on the day their petition was presented to the House of Commons to say that the Arun proprietors did not 'mean in any way to interfere with Lord Egremont's navigation and that the present application is to extend their navigation from Arfold (Orfold) Lock to Lee Bridge in Kirdford'.

Even so, Henry advised his brother that great care and circumspection were necessary on the part of his lordship during the progress of this bill through the two Houses. 'I think we know enough of the Arun proprietors to be assured that they may say one thing and mean another.' Henry continued:

These things make it extremely important to watch them with due care and they impress my mind very favourably with the necessity of the personal attendance of someone on the part of his lordship, understanding the relative interests of both of the parties and capable to give immediate notice of any clause which they may smuggle into their own bill, if not narrowly watched, affecting immediately and directly his lordship's plan.

Henry Tripp was soon proved right. The Arun proprietors not only petitioned the House of Commons on 28 February 1792 for an Act to extend their navigation from Orfold to Kirdford, but they had also included in the petition a request for powers to continue the cutting from Hardham Tunnel to the Rother Navigation above Stopham Lock.

The reason why the Arun proprietors had had to resort to this ruse was the simple fact that they were losing money because the bargemasters were unwilling to pay the shilling-a-ton toll to use the tunnel, when for the sake of an extra six hours they could, if they had a light load, use the old river by Pulborough toll free – a stretch of navigation which, under the terms of their Act, the Arun proprietors had to maintain at their expense and which, by doing so, robbed them of their income – or so they claimed. Inducements introduced in 1789 to encourage traders to use the tunnel by offering toll-free passage if their barges deposited or took up goods from the company's wharves⋆ had met with little response.[61]

To overcome this legitimate means of avoiding toll fees, the Arun proprietors proposed to continue the Coldwaltham Cut beyond Hardham Tunnel to the Rother above Stopham Lock. However, what seemed a time-saving proposal to save boats bound to and from Midhurst from locking up and down, was really a device to encourage greater use of the tunnel and to make it more difficult for the Rother barges to avoid paying toll. The treasurer was authorized to borrow £2,500 for these works at the committee meeting held on 28 February 1792.

Yet Lord Egremont must have already been aware of the Arun's intentions and the puzzle is why no attempt was made to reach an agreement over the problem. Egremont acted by asking William Tyler, his Petworth attorney, to check whether the standing orders of the House relating to private bills had been observed. Tyler replied that he, along with Mr Smyth, the Uptons and Jones the contractor, had been at Stopham and 'that they found that the Arun proprietors could in fact make their cut by two different courses without touching on Coldwaltham or any parishes other than Hardham and Stopham, the only parishes named in the petition'. Twelve landowners were listed along the proposed line of the Kirdford Canal, but apparently such a list was omitted for the Stopham Cut. It was indeed this failure to comply with standing orders which prevented the bill's further progress.

⋆ Houghton, Watersfield, Stopham, Pallingham and Newbridge.

The entrance to Hardham Lock, 1889.

The north end of Hardham Tunnel, 1843. Observe the crude tree trunks used as beams for opening the gates of Tunnel Lock.

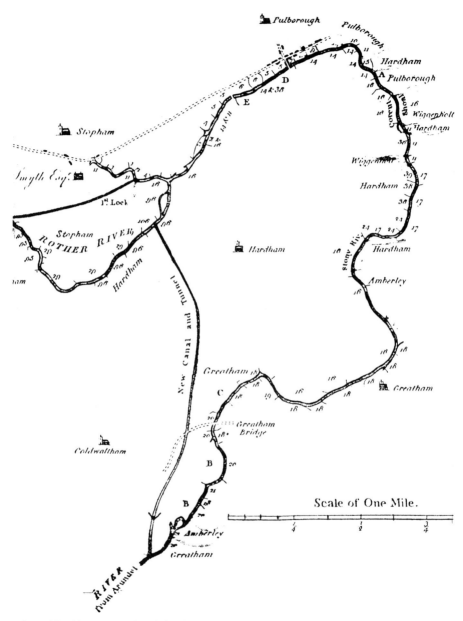

The Coldwaltham Cut reduced the distance between Arundel and Midhurst by water by over 3 miles. The length of Hardham Tunnel was 375 yards.

Knowledge of how to present a petition and obtain a private Act of Parliament was little known outside the legal profession and Westminster. Even less known was what could be done to oppose one, always assuming that one was aware of what was happening. The need for a watchful parliamentary agent was therefore just as important in 1792 as it is today. The insertion of an extra clause could easily pass unnoticed and adherence to standing orders was not always too closely observed. In spite of new requirements for the introduction of private bills introduced in 1794, criticisms were being levelled at the way private bills could be introduced fifty years later. Coincidentally, it was the clerk to the Arun Navigation who wrote to the commissioners of the Port of Arundel in 1844: 'I think it is monstrous that the Duke of Norfolk should be favoured and placed in a position different from the mass. I really believe that there is more injury inflicted by private bills in one year than by general laws in six.'[62]

The arguments presented by Egremont in his petition against the Arun proprietors' bill were that firstly he would lose tolls calculated at 3s 8d on every 30-ton load of timber or coal (in other words the toll of 3d a ton-mile for 860 yards); secondly that if at any time their banks or locks were at fault, requiring the water to be lowered for their repair, his trade on the Rother would be entirely stopped; thirdly that the navigation of the River Arun between Stopham and Greatham had been materially hurt by opening the lock sluices at Coldwaltham to draw water from the River Rother in dry times to allow barges to pass through the tunnel.[63] The earl felt very strongly about this latter point.

At the quarterly meeting of the proprietors of the Arun Navigation on 1 March 1792, it was reported that they had already spent more than £16,000 and that they considered his lordship's navigation 'as a rival interest to theirs and as the principal cause of their present failure'.

As the Rother Navigation was not yet open, the comment that it was the cause of their present failure needs further examination. The Arun Navigation had been completed during the summer of 1790 and tolls collected during the twelve months to July 1791, the first full year of operation, totalled £856, representing some 14,000 tons of cargo. This was less than half what had been anticipated and the winter of 1791/2 saw a further slight fall compared with the previous year.

There is no record of the Arun proprietors having consulted Lord Egremont about the Kirdford Canal, nor indeed was it necessary to do more than ascertain whether the owners and occupiers assented or dissented to the scheme. But it seems extraordinary that they should have included in their petition powers to make a collateral cut which would clearly affect Lord Egremont's navigation, not only without consulting Lord Egremont, but deliberately misinforming him that their petition only sought powers for the Kirdford Canal. One can only conclude that this degree of antipathy towards his lordship was occasioned, not just by the simple fact that they believed his navigation was detrimental to the success of their own (because he was encouraging the use of the old river via Pulborough rather than through Hardham Tunnel), but to a large degree by the different outlooks, on the one hand, of a very wealthy landowner seeking the public good, and on the other, of the local merchants who were naturally more influenced by the profit motive and who had only received an annual return on their original investment of less than $1\frac{1}{2}$ per cent over a period of ten years. The loss to Lord Egremont's navigation would have been minimal and if cordial relations could have been established a form of compensation should not have been difficult to reach. In due course, the House of Commons rejected the petition 'for want of the Arun Navigation proprietors' obedience to the orders of this House's provisions to their carrying in their petition'.

The Arun proprietors' proposals would have been of public benefit since, besides providing the Wisborough Green and Kirdford area with water communication, it would have enabled barges going to Midhurst and using the tunnel to avoid passing through Hardham and Stopham locks. It would have certainly encouraged traffic to use the tunnel since the distance between Houghton and Coultershaw Wharf, Petworth, would have been reduced to $6\frac{1}{2}$ miles instead of 10 by the old river. Equally, however, the people of Pulborough required some guarantee that the navigation would be properly maintained and this, it was noted, had not been done.

There is one other matter which may be relevant. It is the building of Clements Bridge in the late 1790s or early 1800s (see SNQ XVI pp. 233–4). This triple-arched stone bridge crossed the Arun above the railway bridge at Pulborough.★ Its origin remains unknown. It is not mentioned in Jessop's reports. It carried no highway and was only used by cattle, yet its headroom and the river's draught prevented all but lightly laden barges from proceeding above Pulborough to the Rother Navigation. Yet there is no record of complaints from Lord Egremont or the bargemasters who had necessarily to use the tunnel when the river was either high or low. Was there, perhaps, an understanding between the Mr Clement who built the bridge (he was a yeoman of Pulborough) and the Arun proprietors, and did Lord Egremont, after he became chief shareholder of the Arun Navigation, reach a

---

★ Clements Bridge was swept away by flood water in the early morning of 16 September 1968. The river authority removed the ruined piers and used the stone to raise the river wall at Templemead below Swan Bridge, Pulborough.

Clements Bridge, Pulborough (drawn here in 1843) was built in the late 1790s or early 1800s. Its ostensible purpose was to provide access to the meadows for cattle; however, its low arches suggest that its main object was to discourage barges using the toll-free river instead of Hardham Tunnel. Pulborough Church tower is upper left.

compromise with the users of the Rother Navigation by reducing the tunnel toll?

Attempts were also made to extend the Arun Canal as far as Horsham. On 9 July 1792 a well-attended meeting was held at the Town Hall, Horsham, under the chairmanship of the Duke of Norfolk, when it was resolved to make the Arun navigable from Newbridge to Weald Cross, Slinfold. Later it was agreed to extend the terminus a mile further to Farthing Bridge on the Guildford-Horsham turnpike, less than a mile from the centre of the town. It was argued in favour of the scheme that it would improve the agricultural value of the lands and estates adjoining the river, which suffered from continual flooding, and that it would bring great benefits to the trade and commerce of Horsham.

The survey carried out by John Rennie showed the scheme to be practicable, the cost was estimated at £18,133 and leave to bring in a bill was granted by the House of Lords in February 1793. Over £15,000 had already been subscribed when, following a series of meetings, the committee formed to carry through the project found tht they could reach no satisfactory agreement with the proprietors of the Arun Navigation, even though the promoters offered to pay the Arun Navigation 75 per cent of the maximum tunnel toll and either to purchase the Arun Canal at cost price or that reduced tolls should be levied when the Arun Navigation's profits exceeded 10 per cent.

The short-sightedness of the Arun proprietors over the concessions and working arrangements, which had led to the collapse of the plan to extend the Arun Canal to Horsham, had incensed Egremont even more and it was doubtless their attitude which prompted Young to say that the great advantage of the Rother Navigation being in the hands of one owner was that he 'feels a greater spur in the success of it' than any company of merchants who live at a distance and subscribe their money. By vesting the undertaking in the hands of an individual, no opposition is likely to be met with; nor is the business liable to be thwarted or counteracted.'[64]

As will be related Lord Egremont now realized that as Sir Harry Goring, the Chairman of the Arun Navigation and owner of the land in Wisborough Green through which any canal to London via Guildford or Horsham would have to pass, was opposed to the scheme, negotiations had to be continued. In this respect he was assisted by the Arun's parlous financial state. Not even the proprietors found it possible to pay those responsible for managing the navigation, and in December 1793 it was resolved that 'the late Henry Digance and Thomas Seward be compensated for the time and trouble in superintending the works of the navigation by the issue of two shares each'.[65]

Although toll receipts were satisfactory, nothing had been done to reduce the company's huge mortgage, which was more than the original capital subscribed, with the result that interest charges accounted for half the revenue. The company was reluctant to take action and proposals to suspend dividend payments (which had been paid at a rate of from 2 to 4 per cent between 1792 and 1796) were ill-received by some of the proprietors.

At length, and only after some considerable hesitation due to personal animosity, it was decided in June 1796 'to allow Lord Egremont to subscribe to the outstanding twenty-six shares at par on condition that he would lend his support to promoting the bill for the extension of the navigation to Horsham'.[66] Moreover, it was an additional condition that Egremont would purchase at par any Arun shares which holders might wish to sell within the next ten years. Sir Harry Goring resigned the chairmanship in favour of the earl, to whom he also sold his shareholding, thus giving Egremont 36 per cent of the company's capital. The company's first action was to redeem £2,450 of mortgage bonds, but resolutions not to declare dividends until the debt had been considerably reduced were adjourned until 1800, though none were in fact paid after 1796 until 1821.

Egremont's main concern in all his enterprises was to improve standards. His enlightened disinterest in the profit motive is best illustrated in a letter he wrote in 1812, at a time when he was actively supporting the Wey & Arun Junction Canal bill, in which he opposed the revival of schemes to make the Yorkshire Ouse and Swale rivers navigable in Acts passed in 1767:

The acts passed forty-five years ago were intended . . . for public benefit and not for private emolument. They gave power to subscribers to execute that public benefit and to levy tolls as proper remuneration for the money expended; and the subscribers on their part contracted an obligation with the public to carry that benefit into execution. The acts have been in force during many years of the peace succeeding the Seven Years War when the rate of interest was lowest, and during the last fourteen years, when the circulation of paper money arising from the restriction of bank cash payments has given such facility to speculations of internal improvement, that the attention of Parliament has lately been almost as much employed in watching and checking useless and improvident projects as in forwarding those which are useful and good. And now, at the end of these forty-five years, the part of the objects of these acts which has been executed is so inconsiderable that it bears no proportion to the original plan or to the just expectations of the public.[67]

To Egremont, the canalization of the Rother meant improving the trading facilities and living conditions of the locality, and was specified in the Act as being for the repayment of money laid out by the promoter. The maximum toll allowed on coal, corn, timber and general merchandise was 3*d* a ton mile. This represented a charge of 3*s* a ton for the 12 miles from Stopham to Midhurst and was the rate charged from the opening of the navigation until the Wey & Arun Junction Canal was opened, when some reductions were allowed on traffic to London. Chalk was always charged at less than the maximum rate of 1*d* a ton mile (see page 106).

CHAPTER SIX

THE PETWORTH CANAL (1795–1826)

The first attempt to reach London – William Jessop's opinion – Thomas Upton surveys a line to Guildford and Horsham (1793) – negotiations with the Wey Navigation (1793) – building of the Petworth Canal to Haslingbourne Bridge – opened in 1795 – its cost – extension intended to Hampers Common – Upton's estimate – Petworth to Duncton Hill Turnpike Act (1800) – Rotherbridge pulled down – coal traffic in 1820 – Petworth Canal closed and the locks demolished (1826).

The building of the Petworth Canal was the first step towards the realization of the Earl of Egremont's plan to link the Rother Navigation to the Thames. As Young recorded in the 1790s, 'by a direct communication from Petworth to Guildford, by a collateral branch to Horsham, a very considerable proportion of the county would be benefited'.

William Jessop carried out a preliminary survey in August 1790 and reported that he had seen 'as much of the country between the rivers Rother and Wey as to enable me to say it is practicable to make a navigable communication between the two rivers'. After drawing attention to the fact that it would at all events exceed the ordinary expense of similar undertakings, he optimistically considered it would pay its way. 'I am much inclined to believe that if executed, there would be trade upon it to pay interest for the expense.'[68]

Jessop added that it 'would indisputably increase the value of property in the neighbourhood'. Nevertheless, he advised Lord Egremont not to pursue this idea for the moment since 'it is a business much too complicated to admit of due investigation before the ensuing Session of Parliament', but to instruct Mr Upton to make further enquiries and 'to permit him at his leisure to spend a few weeks in taking the levels of the country'. Jessop was confident that an adequate water supply could be found, 'there are living waters to be procured at a sufficient height to supply the summit,' but warned that they must be purchased from the mill-owners who now possessed them. Again he advised that it might be cheaper to build reservoirs for 'reclaiming winter waters' and thereby avoid 'that perplexing opposition which is sure to arise from mill-owners. While Mr Upton is searching the country he will keep that object in view; if he cannot find ground enough for the whole, he may for part of it.'*

During the late spring and summer of 1793 Thomas Upton 'roughly' surveyed the country between Petworth and Guildford. He then produced two options. The first was to extend the Petworth Canal some 32 miles to Shalford where the River Wey was already open for navigation from Godalming to the Thames. The proposed line would have passed through North Chapel, Shillinglee Park and Dunsfold to Alfold. From this village the Godalming Navigation would be reached by following the valley of the Cranleigh stream through Bramley to Shalford. The lockage was estimated at 220 ft. The second proposal was to dig a 9-mile lockless collateral branch canal from Alfold to Rudgwick and Broadbridge Heath, which could be extended to Horsham. Upton also suggested that an easier solution would be for the Arun Canal to be continued some 17 miles to Shalford, following a line that Josias Jessop was to recommend in 1811.[69]

Thus in 1793, the year when the canal mania was at its height, Lord Egremont was faced with a conflicting set of options. He could push ahead with his plan to extend the Petworth Canal (which had yet to be started) to either Shalford or Horsham (from Horsham there were plans for the Dorking Canal to pass through Mole Valley to the Thames).† Alternatively he could try to come to some arrangement with the Arun Navigation and support proposals to extend their canal from Newbridge. However, his opposition to their attempt to encourage barges to use the tunnel cut as well as the differences of opinion between them did not hold out much promise of their reaching any prompt agreement.

Lord Egremont's efforts to come to some arrangement with the joint proprietors of the Wey Navigation (Bennet Langton‡ and the Earl of

---

* It was indeed the lack of water on the summit that limited the success of the Wey & Arun Junction Canal during the 1830s.

† At a meeting held in Horsham on 12 January 1793 it was resolved that a survey should be made to determine the best line from either Newbridge or Shoreham to Dorking, a survey from Dorking to Thames Ditton having already been made.

‡ In 1770 Bennet Langton (1737–1801) of Langton, Lincolnshire, had married the widowed Countess of Rothes, who had inherited half the Wey Navigation from her husband. From early middle age Langton had settled into the life of a country landowner, spending long periods with Boswell, Johnson and other members of the Literary Club in London. Indeed he had known Dr Johnson since his undergraduate days at Oxford. He was famous for his Greek scholarship and became professor of ancient literature at the Royal Academy in 1788.

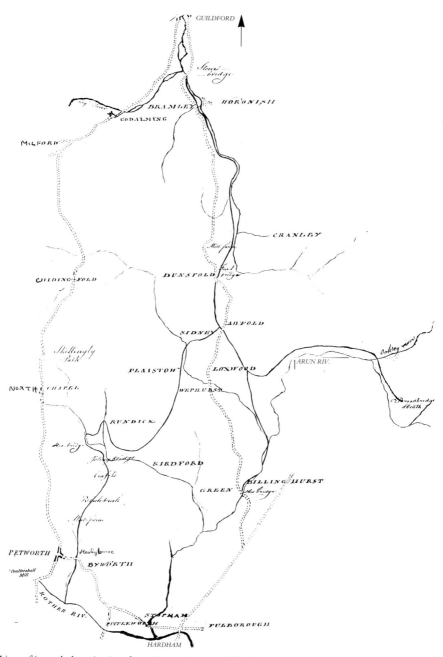

Line of intended navigation from Petworth to Guildford with branches to Horsham and Newbridge, 1793.

Portmore⋆) also met with a negative response. John Granger, the Wey Navigation's agent wrote that 'he was entirely adverse, as the lowering of the toll on goods navigated on a canal from Petworth to Godalming must of course be followed up in making the same abatement for all goods to be navigated to and from Godalming to London. Therefore I am persuaded in my own mind that it would be very injudicious to make any abatement whatever by reason of its commencing at the head of the Wey river.'[70]

In September Lord Egremont asked George Stubbs,† the Wey Navigation's attorney, to call at his London house to discuss his proposals and the need for toll reductions on through traffic from the Thames to Petworth. Stubbs reported to the partners, who were unable to meet as Langton was away at Warley with the North Lincoln Militia in which he was a major. Lord Portmore, however, wrote to Langton remarking that while both he and Stubbs were in a better position to judge the business, he, Portmore, considered it would be very dangerous to lower the tolls. He also felt that while attention must be paid to any new navigation which might hurt theirs, 'I think it should be attended with as little expense as possible and, unless absolutely necessary, should be avoided. I advise this, that our future quarters [toll receipts] may not be hurt. I should be glad to avoid as far as is proper any expenses as to Thames Locks as this has been a very expensive spring to me.'

In spite of the uncertainties Lord Egremont ordered work to begin on the Petworth Canal. The branch to Haslingbourne left the Rother a little upstream of the artificial cut to Shopham Lock. The surface width was to be only 20 ft. Thomas Upton notes in 1795 'to altering the passing place as my lord directs', which indicates that the canal was built for single-line traffic. The two locks were each to have a rise of 8 ft 6 in and to be built of ashlar and rough stone quarried from the pits at Byworth and Pitshill.

Preparatory work began in the late autumn of 1794, when a road was made to the site of the lower lock (Hains) and a temporary bridge built over the Haslingbourne stream. Digging began in the new year and was in full swing between the two locks in March 1795 when some twenty navvies were at work. In May Lord Egremont decided to alter the site of one of the winding holes, lock cills were put in at Hains, a 'pile engine' was barged from

---

⋆ William Colyear, the 3rd Earl of Portmore (1745–1822), had succeeded his father in 1785. In 1770 he had married the daughter of the Earl of Rothes, Lady Mary Leslie, who had inherited the other half of the Wey Navigation. The 3rd earl had a reputation for being irascible and of a violent temper. His father had left the family property entangled with mortgages and other debts which made the earl particularly unwilling to risk any venture which might reduce his income from the Wey Navigation.

† Stubbs was also much involved with the management of the Basingstoke Canal between 1787 and 1797.

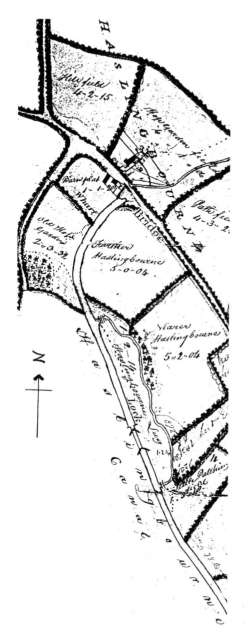

An 1806 field plan showing the terminus of the Petworth Canal at Haslingbourne Bridge. The bed of the old stream can be seen to the east of the lock.

Midhurst and planks from Todham. In June a tow-path bridge was built over the brook below Upper Lock and a horse bridge across the middle pound. In July William Jessop was invited down to Petworth again to 'view the course of a canal from Petworth to Guildford and Littlehampton Harbour'. The only extant document relating to his visit is a sketch of the line to be adopted from Haslingbourne Bridge to Shalford, with a branch from Alfold to Horsham. In August the lock-gates were being hung, and a lock-bridge built at Hains to which spot 22 tons of very large ashlar coping was barged by Edmund Sayer from Todham and Moorland locks. By October 1795 Haslingbourne Wharf was serviceable and the navigation open.

The cost of building the Petworth Canal was £4,980, of which £2,200 was for labour and materials and £2,780 for the purchase of land and damages. The total amount expended on the Rother Navigation by the end of 1796 was £18,280 from which sum £1,624 can be deducted, being tolls received. The authorized capital of the Arun Navigation was £10,000 and it had cost £16,000 to complete.[71] When the moment comes to assess the profitability of each navigation, it is fair to assume that if the Rother Navigation had been floated as a public company its share capital would most likely have been the same as that of the Arun.

Lord Egremont now gave serious attention to Upton's estimate for building the next section – a 2¼-mile canal from Haslingbourne to Long Mead by Hampers Common on the north-east side of Petworth. The figures were not encouraging. As many as nine locks were proposed to raise the canal 58 ft. At Hampers Common a basin was to be sited to the south of Northland Farm, about 800 yards north of the lane which was to become the Petworth-Wisborough Green turnpike in 1823 (now the A272). The water supply was to come from the brook leading out of Noar Upper Pond. Six bridges (two road at Haslingbourne and Shimmins, one hunting, one foot and three occupational) and a second wharf and basin by Shimmins Bridge were also planned as well as the excavation of 3,982 cubic yards of earth.★ Lord Egremont wondered whether the extensive lockage and the cost, estimated at £8,256, could be justified. Arthur Young explained the benefits. As farmers around Petworth required 80 to 120 bushels of manure per acre of wheat, the intended canal would enable wagons to be loaded with chalk from the Arun Valley at Hampers Common instead of at Duncton, and so allow them to collect three or four loads instead of one in

---

★ Although parliamentary powers were not sought for this extension, a study of the upper reaches of the Rectory Brook (or Haslingbourne stream) suggests that some work may have been started in making cuts and weirs. It was the intention to build locks at Haslingbourne Bridge, Bushey Leith, Byworth, Shimmins (4), Goa (Gohanna) and Flatt Field.

The toll-gate at Coultershaw, c. 1860. The house was built from stone taken from the bridge that had spanned the river at Rotherbridge. It was probably completed in 1802 and was demolished in the late 1870s. The foundations were visible on the west side of the canal bridge in the 1950s.

a day.[72] This argument does not, and presumably did not, sound very convincing as farmers could already collect chalk from Coultershaw or Rotherbridge. But what now became obvious to his lordship was that the lockage required to cross the watershed into Surrey was going to be very considerable.* Another route had to be found and the one from Newbridge to Shalford looked more promising.

Thus Lord Egremont abandoned his plan to extend the Petworth Canal, as recorded in Chapter Five, and reached an agreement with the Arun Navigation proprietors in June 1796 allowing him to subscribe to the Arun's outstanding share capital on condition that he lent his support to promoting the bill for the extension of the Arun Canal to Horsham.[73] However, no sooner was this agreed than the economic problems arising from the war with France halted waterway development throughout the kingdom, and plans to link the Thames to the English Channel remained dormant until the turn of the century.

---

* The actual lockage between Newbridge and Shalford was 167 ft or some 55 ft less than that estimated by Thomas Upton for a route between Petworth and Shalford.

A photograph of the entrance to Hungers Lane by Walter Kevis taken about the turn of the century. Before the demolition of Rotherbridge in 1800 travellers passed this way to Tillington whereas those using the turnpike went by Cross Lane to Petworth.

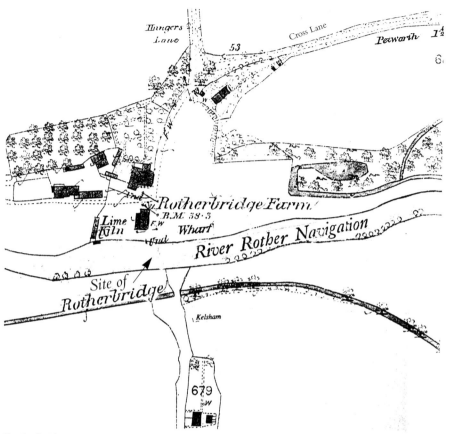

Rotherbridge was the site of the double-arched stone bridge built by Parson Acon in the late fourteenth century and demolished in 1800 when a new bridge was erected at Coultershaw. There was no replacement, as this 1875 map shows, until the 1890s, when, after barge traffic had ceased, a floating foot-bridge was erected to allow access from Kelsham to Hungers Lane.

Until 1800 the turnpike road from Milford to Petworth and the top of Duncton Hill passed by Rotherbridge. John Leland (1506–52), the antiquarian, recorded that it was 'a fayre Bridge of Stone made by one Parson Acon', who had also built the spire to the lead steeple of Petworth Church. However, the Petworth Turnpike Trustees, which included Lord Egremont, suspected William Warren, the miller at Coultershaw, of allowing his 'friends' to avoid the toll by using the mill bridge. Egremont solved the problem by offering to build a new road up to Heath End, an offer which the trustees accepted in November 1798. This paved the way for the 1800 Act to be passed, which authorized the extension of the turnpike from Duncton to Chichester and its re-routing by Coultershaw Mill instead of by Rotherbridge.[74] The twin-arched bridge there was pulled down and the stone used to build a new bridge at Coultershaw with a toll-gate on the west side of the river.[75] The old road by Rotherbridge and up Cross Lane or Hungers Lane had been termed 'devious, narrow and incommodious'. Hungers Lane can still be followed today as a bridle path, cut in places through beds of sandstone, leading from the foot-bridge over the Rother to Tillington. The navigation accounts make only one reference to the bridge being taken down in an entry dated April 1801: 'W. Duff & Son for boating 3 loads of stone from Rotherbridge to Lodsbridge Wharf to mend the road at the gateway including digging a small part out of the old foundation, the remainder was refuse left from the old bridge'.★

The Petworth Canal never carried much traffic. What it did carry was principally chalk and coal up and lime and timber down. Reference is also made to bark and spokes being loaded at Haslingbourne.[76] However, the total traffic never amounted to much, reaching at most 500 or 600 tons in any one year. The only figures available relate to 1820 when $174\frac{1}{4}$ tons of coal went up to the wharf by the mill below Haslingbourne Bridge compared with $535\frac{3}{4}$ tons to Rotherbridge Wharf and 1,683 tons to Coultershaw.

There is little of great import to record in the canal's thirty or so years of operation. A lime-kiln was established near Richard Marshall's barnyard, where in 1802 two gates had to be hung at the wharf entrance. In December 1801 a chalk barge tore up the forebay and cill of Upper Lock, and between August and September 1802 eight boatloads (763 bushels) of lime were fetched from Haslingbourne for the rebuilding of Moorland Lock. In November 1805 it was further reported that 60 tons of spoil was laid 'in Mr Marshall's lagg (sic) by the lime-kiln'. In April 1806 timber was boated down the canal to Fittleworth for use by Charles Bridger, the lock-carpenter.

The cut was regularly maintained. In 1805, 480 tons of soil were dredged from the upper pound and 300 from the middle pound. In 1808 Bridger fitted a new balance beam to the lower gates of Upper Lock. Ten years later the locks were fitted with new paddles and the stonework refaced. In 1821 the wooden bridge over the brook by Hains Lock was repaired. During 1825 the ballast barge, under the direction of William Moor, dredged 280 tons which was used to repair the banks.

The following year it was reported to his lordship that both Stopham and Fittleworth locks were in need of urgent attention. Lord Egremont's interest

---

★ F.W. Arnold, writing in 1864, stated that the remains of the bridge could still be seen when the water was low. (*Petworth – a sketch of its History and Antiquities*, p. 75)

The bed of the Petworth Canal after heavy rain in 1963. The canal was filled in by Lord Egremont after its closure in 1826. The tithe map of 1838 showed only a short stretch of water and the land here has now been levelled; however, the upper reaches can be traced by observing where the Haslingbourne stream was straightened below the bridge.

in waterways must have been at a low ebb. His lordship had just decided to surrender his holding of 315 shares in the Portsmouth & Arundel Canal (issued at £15,750), which was proving a disaster, to pay the company's debt of £40,000 due to the government which he had guaranteed,[77] and to announce that he would abandon any claim for its future reimbursement. Feeling perhaps that he had had enough problems with waterways, he now decided, in view of its limited use, to close the Petworth Canal and to use the materials from the locks to repair those on the Rother. It is doubtful if any consideration was given to the obligation required by the Act of Parliament to maintain the canal as a public navigation.

In July James Boxall spent six and a half days taking down the woodwork of Upper Lock. During August thirty workmen dismantled Hains Lock and removed the stonework of both locks, which was used in rebuilding the locks on the Rother. New gates were fitted, and a pair removed from Upper Lock were rehung, at Fittleworth. Work was then begun on partially restoring the Haslingbourne stream to its former channel and to filling in the canal between the two locks.

Over the years evidence of the former waterway has all but vanished. The tithe award map of Petworth reveals that by 1838 only 300 yards of the channel from its junction with the river remained and that the former bed across Rough Meadow, Hough Brook and Brook Field, where Hains Lock was sited, had been levelled.

Today's countryside explorer will find only a shallow depression near Hains Lock, which fills with water after heavy rain. Above this point the Haslingbourne stream flows down the line of the old waterway, while swampy areas on either side indicate where the sinuosities of the original stream were dissected when the canal was cut. There is no trace of the wharf at Haslingbourne. The narrowness of the brook here and below Hampers Common shows to a surprising extent how even a small stream could, in 1793, provide both William Jessop and Lord Egremont with enough optimism to contemplate seriously its forming a waterway to London.

CHAPTER SEVEN

BARGE TRAFFIC (1796–1816)

*The management of the Rother Navigation – Thomas Upton, the superintendent –
John King, the collector of tolls – the principal cargoes – the development of the
Houghton Chalk Pits – the brig* Egremont *– the timber trade – the local carriers –
the barge-owners – John Ibbetson of Arundel – William Stoveld – Coultershaw Wharf
– William Smith, the wharfinger at Midhurst – maintenance and the ballast barge –
toll receipts and tonnage.*

Lord Egremont delegated the day-to-day running of the navigation to
Thomas Poling Upton (1763–1845). Thomas was a surveyor who came from
a well-known and respected Petworth family. It was Upton who had had sole
responsibility for the navigation since the Jones's had departed and whose
efficiency and attention to detail had ensured the successful completion of the
waterway.

Upton's accounts,[78] which had to be seen by William Tyler (who had
succeeded Tripp as Lord Egremont's Sussex agent in 1800) before being
passed to his lordship for approval, were a model of detail and accuracy. They
contained the names of every workman employed, the days he worked and his
rate of pay. There were no sundry cash payments. Every item of expenditure,
however small, was listed. Sixpence was spent on mending a pail, 4*d* a hook,
3*s* for purchasing a sieve, 2*s* for a bucket. A mop, broom and tiver★ for the
lock-carpenter was 10½*d*. Many entries reflect Upton's sensible methods of
getting things done. 'Gave miller at Stedham 2*s* for drink for lowering the
water'; 'Gave carters 2*s* for drink, having some difficulty to get over Moorland
new bridge with hay, (the bridge) not being quite backed'; 'Gave the
workmen 5*s* for beer on account for working nights when the water was
drawed down in the day'.

There were other nice touches: 'Gave Robert Russel, the lock-carpenter
who was ill and could not work for six weeks, two guineas by my lord's
orders'.

As all boats using the Rother Navigation had to return the same way, it was

---

★ A red colouring matter used for marking sheep and timber.

agreed that only one toll collector was necessary and that he should be based at Fittleworth since there was virtually no traffic passing Stopham Lock which did not tie up or proceed beyond Fittleworth Wharf.★

The printed ledgers kept by the collector contained no less than twelve ruled columns. Each horizontal entry indicated the date, the name of the owner, the registered number of the barge, the kind of lading, its weight, its origin, its destination, the distance to the nearest furlong and the toll and wharfage charges.

Until the opening of the Wey & Arun Junction Canal in 1816, traffic was relatively light. On average there were only two barges a week in winter and ten in the summer. April, May, June and September were normally the busiest months when the river had the greatest draught, was free from weeds and suffered least from drought and floods. River navigations were as subject as canals to the severe vagaries of the British climate; floods were the biggest impediment but ice also could be a problem when the lock cuts were frozen over and the lock-gates jammed, sometimes for weeks on end.

John King, who lived with his family in Lower Street, was appointed collector of tolls in 1793 at a salary of £15 per annum increased to £20 in 1794. He also acted as lock-keeper and wharfinger. During the next twenty-five years his name crops up frequently in the daily affairs of the navigation. In 1804 he was given 10s for a new ledger and alphabet and provided with a little boat costing £3 to enable him to reach Stopham floodgates when the meadows were awash. In 1806 the boat was swept away by the floods and sunk opposite Greatham Farm. To avoid this happening again King was paid 2s 8d for a padlock. He also received two guineas for conscientiously giving information about Mr Smyth's breach of the by-laws in raising the paddles of Stopham Lock to allow the flood water through. King was a yeoman and his wife Mary bore him at least one son, Charles Phillip born in 1808. When the lock-keeper was away from home, it was Mary or his servants Ann Rice or Charity Cearn who let the barges through and who were told by the bargemasters the nature and weight of their cargoes. They in turn told Mr King on his return; sometimes the maid servants reported the details to their mistress and she then reported all to her husband.

The toll collector's job had its problems especially when some of the bargemasters tried to find ways to evade the proper dues. William Upton, the Petworth merchant, informed King that he was not to trust any bargemaster, who was carrying his goods, to pass without paying unless they were in his

---

★ The ledgers reveal that in 1843 one cargo was unloaded at Coates. There were probably other occasions.

own barges. This was easier said than done. One day bargee George Smart came along in no. 17 carrying Upton's goods and King refused to let him pass. 'The man begged hard as he had no money', but King was firm and after a while went away leaving the lock fastened. However, some minutes later, the lock-keeper 'saw the horse and found the man was got through' and that the lock had been left full and not drawn. Correspondence with the barge-owner produced a letter of apology and payment of recompense.

There is some evidence that King could be petty minded, although the incident in question occurred only a few months before his death, and in any case William Stoveld's past behaviour (see Chapter Eight) probably justified the toll collector's attitude. Stoveld complained about the way King was calculating the toll on his barges, 'if it so happened that a barge should have some other goods in besides timber'. Stoveld went on to recount how not long ago 'his barge no. 78, with William Strudwick in command had been loaded with timber at Lodsbridge and had then taken in upon the timber 27 bundles of hoops which did not weigh more than a ton'. When Strudwick got to Fittleworth, King would not let him go through without paying toll by weight for the whole. 'I then ordered the bargemen to take out the hoops and pay for the tonnage of them by weight and the timber by measurement which King would not consent to, but made me pay for the whole by weight – about 7s 6d more than his lordship's due'. Stoveld went on to complain that King 'takes for a quarter of a ton which the index of the barges do not show neither can he tell whether there is a quarter of a ton in or not; nor do they take it on any other river'.[79]

There was another incident in July 1818 when the Arundel Lighter Company complained that King refused to let their 'branch' barge through to Petworth and Midhurst because although the name Monk & Co. was marked on the gunwales, the names of all the proprietors, as required by the Act, were missing. Tyler told King that he should let them pass now as they 'seem desirous to do what is right' and he would settle it afterwards.

John King died in 1819, his widow Mary acting in his place for a few months until another John King, who was no relation, took up the post. For some years the basis of the toll collector's remuneration had been altered from a fixed sum to 2½ per cent of the amount collected so that by 1817 the collector was receiving about £30 per annum.

The day-to-day control of the navigation sometimes posed problems since reports of damage or loss of water could take a longer time than was desirable to reach Thomas Upton. Witness the case of Francis Strudwick, master of Stoveld's barge no. 44, who one Friday afternoon in September 1822 had taken down a load of timber from Midhurst Wharf and left up the paddles of both Moorland and Ladymead locks so that the water in Moorland pound 'was quite run out on Saturday morning'. As a result over 200 tons of sand was washed down and the navigation blocked just below Todham Lock.

The chief Sussex industries at the end of the eighteenth century were charcoal and gunpowder. The ironworks had all but vanished. The local manufacturers were a wide range of wooden products varying from axe handles to hoops, woollen fabrics were made at Chichester, paper at Iping and Duncton, and bricks at Harwoods Green and Littlehampton. Potash, made at Bricksill Hill adjoining Petworth, was used by the town's soap masters. Young refers to a brick-kiln near Petworth, which had lately been constructed for supplying the West Indies; 'an open kiln and a dome kiln, each holding 28,000 bricks, they take 30 hours burning with 2,500 bavins at 9s per 100; three men fill in three days and draw in three more. If the demand was brisk, the kiln would burn all the year.' In 1796, 300,000 bricks were made which were sold at 29s per thousand at the yard and for 34s at Arundel.

Chalk, coal and timber were the three commodities for which water transport was most needed and it was chalk which was the key to Lord Egremont's interest in the navigation. His great urge to improve food production made the proper fertilization of land of great importance. Small chalk could be used as manure for lightening and improving the clay soil and large chalk was brought to the kilns for burning with furze to make lime. Until water transport became available the carriage of chalk was an expensive item since 80 to 120 bushels of manure were required for each acre of wheat.[80]

To get the chalk traffic started, Lord Egremont took a ten-year lease on pits at Houghton in June 1794. The initial lessor was Benjamin Brown, and after 1801 the Duke of Norfolk. Egremont placed the pits in charge of Edmund Sayers, who sold the chalk initially at 2s 1½d per freight if being barged up the Rother Navigation or 2s 7½d if destined elsewhere. This low price was intended to cover only the cost of labour. At the same time Lord Egremont fixed the toll on chalk at 3d a ton to any point on the river instead of the maximum rate of 1d a ton mile. While this may have acted as a deterrent to chalk being barged to Fittleworth, it represented a reduction of 33 per cent to Coultershaw and 75 per cent to Midhurst. Lord Egremont was clearly anxious that his tenant farmers should fertilize their land to the greatest possible extent, improve the yield of their crops and, of course, indirectly the value of his estates.

The first barge-loads of large chalk arrived at the kilns at Coultershaw in November 1794, while small chalk which had been carted from Duncton Hanger to Robertsbridge was barged back to Houghton for sale as manure. Between 1795 and 1804 some 2,000 to 3,000 tons of chalk was freighted annually from this one pit, of which about half was taken up the Rother

The chalk pit behind Amberley station. The two barges are lying in the 350 yard cut built by Lord Egremont in 1802 to enable barges to load chalk more easily. The cut was later used in conjunction with the railway (opened in 1863) and was maintained until the outbreak of war in 1914.

Navigation. Around 1800 Lord Egremont decided to cease renting the Houghton Pit★ and to open his own pits. He purchased land at Houghton to the east of what is now Amberley railway station and made a cut 350 yards long from the pits northwards to the River Arun to facilitate the loading of barges. The cut was completed in 1803 at a cost of £400.[81]

Francis Jarrett became tenant and manager of the chalk pits. He built lime-kilns and ran a flourishing barge-carrying business for over twenty years. The rent paid to his lordship was 'merely for the house and land without interest on the capital expenditure'. Not only was chalk barged inland but also coastwise via Arundel. Jarrett also owned the sloop *Hero*, which is recorded in 1819 as carrying 453 tons of chalk to Siddlesham and also to Lord Selsey's estate near West Dean in the Manhood.

★ This operation was finally wound up when the materials left at the chalk pit were sold to Messrs Scarvell & Jarrett on 25 June 1804 at valuation. Francis Jarrett, the lime-burner at Amberley, is not to be confused with Francis Jarrett the younger, who was a grocer at Pulborough.

Houghton Wharf, looking south, *c.* 1905. In the background are the quarries of Pepper & Sons limeworks, which today are the site of the Chalk Pits Museum.

Another impetus to trade was Lord Egremont's decision to enter the coastal trade. In August 1795 he went into partnership with mariner Jeremiah Scarvell junior of Littlehampton. They paid £1,000 for a 141-ton brigantine, newly built at the port, and agreed to share one third of the profits while the captain, who was to provide the crew, was to take two thirds. Scarvell also undertook to bring down annually for his lordship two freights of coal from the north of England at the 'common freight' charge. He also invited the earl to name the ship.

Thus it was the brig *Egremont* which set sail from Littlehampton in August on her first voyage bound for Leith with a cargo of bark; she then went on to Hull with wool and in October returned to Portsmouth with troops. Subsequent voyages were made to London and Dublin with timber. Other cargoes included the biannual delivery of 80 chaldrons of coal from Newcastle to Littlehampton, whence the coal was barged up to Coultershaw.

In November 1797 disaster struck when the *Egremont* was wrecked on the Goodwin Sands. Egremont's half share and the fitting out had cost £802. His share of the profits totalled £281 leaving him with a loss of over £500.

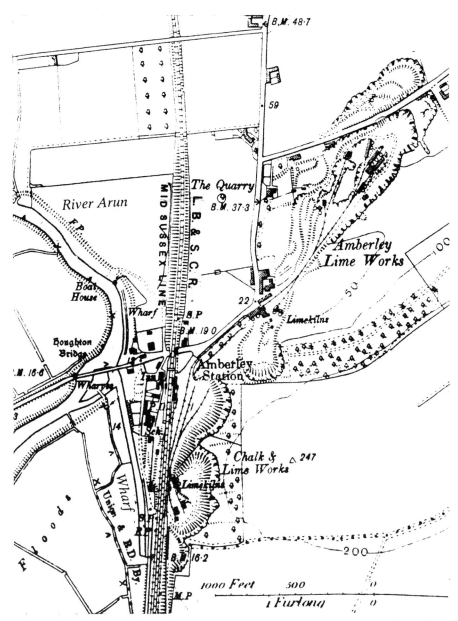

Amberley wharves and chalk pits, 1875. Lord Egremont built a cut 350 yards long from the river south of Houghton Bridge to enable barges to moor as close as possible to the chalk pits he had developed on land he had bought in 1800. Arthur Young reported that the chalk pits supplied some 40,000 tons of chalk a year, much of which was carried up to the kilns on the banks of the Arun and Rother navigations.

NEWCASTLE, *January 19. 1796*

The OWNERS of the SHIP *Egremont* of *Littlehampton*

Mr *Wm Thompson* Master,

To ROBERT LISLE & Co.   Dr.

Name of Pits

Baker For 8 Chaldrons *Byker Coals* — at *15/* £6

Sheriff Hill 9 Ditto *Sheriff Hill Coals* — at *15/* £6

7 Keel Dues — — — at *12/6* 4.13.4

Ditto — — — — — at

7 Keelmen's Beer — — — at *1/4* - 9.4

Spouting — — — — at

Cuftom and Town-Houfe Charges —

Cafh — — — — — 30

Bakers Main 34 Chaldrons *Bakers Main coals 17/* 20.8

Team Coppe 4 Keels *Team & Dues &c* 33.. 5.10

£100..17..6

By Account £28

By Bill in &c Date — 72..17..6 £100..17..6

at 30 Days

CHARGES.

Coast Duty – Ditto Lights – Lows Ditto – Spurn Ditto – Cocket and Bond – Bridlington Pier – Return Ditto – Monthly Bill – Ballast Ticket – Town House – Free Money – Foy

Lord Egremont was joint-owner of the brigantine *Egremont* which often carried coal from the north of England to Littlehampton, whence it was barged up to Petworth. The vessel was wrecked on the Goodwin Sands in 1797.

Most of the coal brought up the Rother Navigation for household use was either imported from Newcastle or the South Wales ports to Arundel where it was discharged into barges. Building materials, slates and, every month or so, groceries and household goods, formed the bulk of the other incoming traffic. Timber was the principal export. The square timber was measured by the foot solid and the 'sawed' timber by the foot superficial. Beech rails were in great demand and these were dispatched all over Britain. William Smith, the wharfinger at Midhurst, stated how they were sent up to Newcastle for the coal trade, being used as rails for the horse-drawn wagons between colliery and landing stage.

The timber traffic embraced every type of wood. Young stated that Lord Egremont's underwoods of oak, beech, alder and willow were cut at twelve to sixteen years of growth and that these small trees were often more profitable than the longer-standing timber since they were in demand for hoops, rails, staves and all manner of wooden utensils as well as hop poles.[82] Hoops and tub staves were required by the coopers for making barrels; spokes and fellies by the carriage trade; bavins and spray faggots were needed in the lime-kilns, cordwood for coaling; bark and firewood were also in great demand. Alder or powderwood made the best charcoal for gunpowder manufacture and this was taken down to Arundel or Littlehampton for shipment by coaster to the factories on the lower reaches of the Thames.

The local land carriers, like Goodman of Midhurst and Dudman of Petworth, played an important role in carting coal from, and timber to, the wharves. Contemporary delivery notes show that oak bark was collected from the local barns, whose names are nowadays often beyond local recall, such as Mr Wetters' barn, Challon barn, Home barn, Upper Lodge as well as from localities like Bepton Common and Easebourne village. Beech planks were brought down from North Park, Kingsleys Coppice, and Delloways Ground on Bepton Common. Trunks of oak and beech were either carted or dragged by strings of horses or oxen from coppices and commons 3, 5 and sometimes 10 miles and more to Midhurst Wharf.

Every barge using the navigation had to be licensed with the name and number painted in large white capital letters and figures on each of the outsides, to which two graduated indices of copper or lead were fixed to denote the tonnage. By the end of 1814 eighty-five barges had been licensed.

The principal trader during the seven year period 1799–1806 was Edward Evershed whose barges made some two hundred voyages annually. Francis Jarrett of Amberley made 34 whereas Lord Egremont's averaged 45 and totalled 179 in 1805 when he increased the size of his fleet. However, by 1805 William Stoveld had become the leading trader who in 1814 was carrying half the navigation's traffic. His fleet of eight barges moved 81 cargoes up and 159

Tree trunks drawn by teams of horses near Midhurst Common, 1898.

cargoes down representing the carriage of 5,425 tons; the largest freight up was 34 and down was 37 tons with the average being 25 tons up and 21½ tons down. The heaviest cargo carried that year was 37 tons of plank from Petworth to Arundel in barge no. 85.

The Rother Navigation was also of great benefit to the townspeople of Petworth and Midhurst and to millers and farmers with wharves on the navigation. However, if land carriage was required to carry goods 3 miles or so to and from the wharves, it was sometimes only marginally more expensive to carry direct to the tidal reaches of the Arun from which point no tolls were payable and carriage charges were less. This position is well illustrated in the correspondence between John Ibbetson of Arundel and Thomas Upton. Previous to the opening of the navigation Ibbetson regularly brought wheat up from Arundel by lighter to Greatham Bridge where he rented a storehouse. From Greatham this cargo was carted to Burton Mill where the wheat was ground into flour and carted back to Greatham. Six horses took two and a half days to move a 10-ton load the 9 miles there and back. With the opening of the navigation, Ibbetson could bring his wheat to the new wharf above Shopham Bridge from where it was carted almost a mile to Burton Mill.★

However, the bargemen charged twice the amount for freight to Shopham Bridge than to Greatham,† and after making two trips there in 1793 Ibbetson wrote to Upton in June drawing attention to his position, the fact that the dues were too high and that they had now reverted to the old method 'and shall no more to Shopham Bridge unless I can agree with Lord Egremont at so much a year'. A further letter written in July included an itemized statement showing that the total additional cost, including freight, tolls and wharfage, of carrying wheat and flour between Greatham and Shopham by water was 2s 8d a ton. Nevertheless, Ibbetson continued to use the navigation for carrying chalk up to Fittleworth, wheat to Shopham and Midhurst, and coal to Midhurst. His only down traffic was flour from Shopham to Arundel.

John Ibbetson must have been quite a character. In 1798 there was some confusion over an outstanding account; Thomas Upton had sent him a statement showing unpaid tolls totalling nearly £5 going back over two years, with a footnote stating 'Lord Egremont has positively resolved that the dues for tonnage and wharfage shall not be in arrears' and at the same time pointing out that a 'much larger sum' was due to him for damages. Ibbetson promptly replied that the account was wrong, 'we do not owe half of it', that Mr King (the toll collector at Fittleworth) had been instructed never to let any barges of his through the lock without paying the dues and that if he (Upton) would 'inquire into our character hope you will find we keep our payments up as close as our neighbours'.

Two years later Ibbetson is still claiming compensation for three years' damages to his water meadows and in a postscript draws attention to the state of Shopham Bridge which prevents him bringing wheat up for grinding at his mill: 'we are going to grind wheat for Mr Horn whose mill is under repair'. Clearly forgetful of his own correspondence of 1793, he complains of having to take the wheat out at Greatham 'which is a great loss; at Shopham I can take it out in a day, at Greatham must be four'.

It was the wharfinger's task to supervise the arrival and departure of all goods arriving by land and water. To the casual observer all would be confusion as his eye roved over the massive piles of 'square' and 'sawed out' timber stacked around the wharf. But the wharfinger knew the nature and

---

★ The mill ceased to grind corn around the turn of the nineteenth century. In 1894 sale particulars described it as having four floors, two overshot water-wheels, four pairs of stones, large corn bins with elevator shoots.

† It is assumed they came via Pulborough to avoid the tunnel dues.

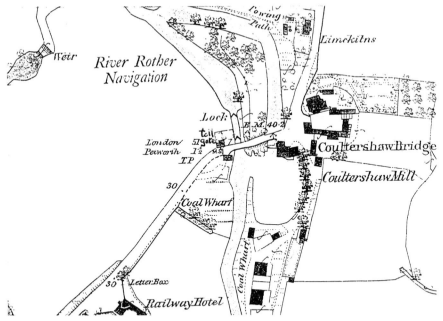

The wharves at Coultershaw served the market town of Petworth and were the busiest on the Rother Navigation. (1875, Ordnance Survey)

size of every lot. There would be huge trunks of trees hewed in rough squares known as 'bodies' and the branches, 'crooks', or if suitable for house or shipbuilding, as 'beams' and 'knees'. Both beams and knees were more valuable. The sawn timber was of great variety and included plank, posts, scantling and rails.

The wharves at Coultershaw were the busiest on the navigation, handling over half the navigation's traffic. By 1808 the wharf stretched out over both sides of the river. 'Big wharf' contained a small warehouse, 30 ft x 16 ft 6 in, leased by William Upton (until 1840), Michael Foard's blacksmiths shop and shoeing shed, also 30 ft long, and six coal pens; a variety of huts and storehouses also stood on 'Little Wharf' which lay on the south bank. Adjacent to the wharf stood Lord Egremont's lime-kilns and William Dale's flour mill. In 1819 an under-wharfinger had to be appointed to assist with the growing traffic.

No salaried wharfinger was employed at Midhurst, but William Smith was paid so much a ton to keep the timber in an orderly manner. However, in December 1796 the confusion at the wharf had become so great that Smith was paid 10*s* to 'him and soldiers for rolling the timber together to make more room in the wharf'. Soldiers were not enough sometimes and it became necessary to employ teams of horses to move the huge trunks of oak and elm strewn around the quayside waiting to be barged down to Arundel. So much timber was there indeed that by 1800 the expense of rolling the timber together to make more room on the wharf exceeded the wharfage dues (receipts totalled £20 2*s* 7½*d* and labour £25 12*s* 2*d*). Upton therefore proposed 'to put two pence more per ton upon the merchants and sink the other penny, and agree with Mr Smith, for three pence per ton for doing the business'. Lord Egremont did not agree, but how the matter was resolved is not stated.

William Smith continued to submit bills for work at Midhurst Wharf until he was succeeded in 1820 by William Goodner, the coal merchant. Goodner rented a coal pen at the basin until 1836. The leading coal merchant and corn dealer in Midhurst was James Monk who also rented a coal pen, 46 ft x 39 ft, as well as a stable and two wagon sheds from 1820 to 1846 (or later) situated on the north-west side of the wharf. In the 1820s Monk & Co. also operated a 'branch' barge to connect with the London and Arundel barges at Stopham.

The ballast barge played an important role in the maintenance of the navigation. Since it had been purchased in 1794, it had been operated by William White and two men. In 1796 it was licensed with the Arun Navigation but no fee appears to have been paid in other years. Not until about 1808 did William Moor take over and he continued the work until 1834 when David Carpenter, who had been employed on the navigation since 1817, replaced him.

Besides the regular work of dredging silt, the ballast barge was essential for repairing the damage caused by what Upton termed 'very great floods', or in one instance, more poetically, 'when the bank was bursted by the great thunder shower'. In 1797 the floods caused sluices to be choked with mud, stone and hay and many banks to be torn asunder. Clay or chalk had to be barged to repair the banks, stone to repair the locks, grit and gravel to mend the towing-path, and 'scrubby' stone to make good holes. Indeed the prosaic details of expenditure reveal the constant trials caused by storm and tempest. Entries like 'for getting up the large boat that was drove away by the flood and sunk and which a team of horses had to drag out' and 'Paid Frank Jarratt one shilling for bringing back a towing-path gate and iron work that was drove away by the flood to Pulborough'. One can picture Edward Sayers and Nathaniel Warner's pleasure in being paid 5*s* for 'getting up Mr King's boat that was drove away and sunk opposite Greatham Farm and bringing it back to Fittleworth'.

In 1800 a new ballast barge was built by Muggeridge for £70 with the old barge taken in part-exchange. Four days were spent replacing the barge tackle and installing a new crane, nets, thongs and mud scoops; then on 15 April there was a small celebration, referred to in the accounts as a 'launch feast' which cost £1 5s.

The basin at Midhurst collected great quantities of silt which had to be dredged regularly; 476 tons were removed during December 1805 and January 1806. Until Pallingham Docks were built in 1804, the ballast barge was taken down to Pulborough for major repairs. In August 1805 White spent six and a half days assisting Samuel Winter in caulking and repairing her at Pallingham, while Thomas Child, the Pulborough blacksmith, did the ironwork.

In 1809 Upton issued instructions on how the barge should be operated. One suspects that the workmen were practising impositions for it was laid down that the barge had to be weighed and marked to show when 20 tons were loaded, that it had to be loaded before dinner and left on the water while the men were at dinner so that checks could be made to see if she was fairly loaded. The men were to receive 3s 3d a week subsistence and were to depart Petworth at six o'clock every morning and not leave their work until four o'clock in the afternoon.

In 1821 the barge had to be extensively overhauled and her 'gudgeon' (a metal pivot) altered. Moor was occupied for thirty-five days taking her to and from Pallingham Docks and 'working with the barge builders repairing her and keeping an account of their time'. James Hill, who assisted Moor with the ballast barge, spent three days in August 1831 fetching 2,000 bricks from Harwoods Green and unloading them at the locks between Stopham and Robertsbridge.

In the early years little capital expenditure was required since the bridges, wharves and weirs were well built and required little attention. However, the constant floods caused damage to the banks, fences, culverts and lock fittings. The lock-carpenter and the ballast barge team had to be always at hand to grease the lock paddles, repair the planking and remove the silt, which rapidly accumulated round the bottom of the gates; equal attention had to be paid to removing the shoals of mud and sand, which appeared after heavy rainfalls, and the repointing of brickwork and masonry. In May 1802, for instance, it took two men, Charles and Daniel Bridger, nine and a half days to grease and turn all the lock tackle and mend the planking and paddles. The following month Moorland Lock had to be partially rebuilt as a result of water in the upper pound getting between the stonework and the rock sand. Not only did the repair cost the substantial sum of £241 14s 2d but traffic was disrupted for ten weeks. There were also contingency items caused by 'mischievous people', who in the winter of 1802, for example, amused themselves by picking out the stones loosened by a settlement in the parapet wall at Lodsbridge and throwing

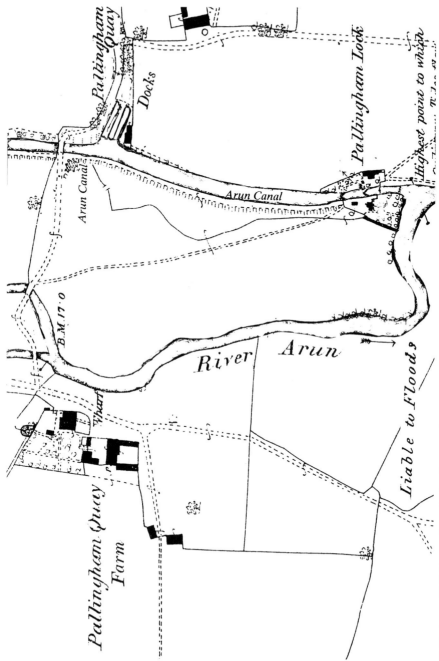

Pallingham, 1875. Barges from the Rother were built and repaired at the docks from 1804 until the 1880s.

them into the river. The estimate for putting the wall in order is marked 'not to be repaired at Lord E's expense without his consent'.

The navigation was proving a success. The reduced cost and facility of freighting coal increased the productivity of the farmers, since it proportionately lessened the demand for furze which had previously had to be grown to provide fuel for the kilns, and so enabled more grain to be sown. Corn, oak-bark, and cordwood for charcoal was being exported in considerable quantities and Young commented that 'by this most useful and public-spirited undertaking many thousand acres of land are necessarily rendered more valuable to the proprietors. Timber is now sent by water. Large falls have been exported which would scarcely have been felled, and the Government Agents and Contractors have made large purchases, in consequence of a more easy communication to the sea. An additional tract of country is also supplied with lime from the Houghton and Bury pits,' the former of which supplied some 40,000 tons annually.

Although initially the navigation's receipts were quite modest, this was partly due to the reduced toll on chalk for which only 3d a ton was charged, whatever the distance, compared with the maximum allowable of 1d a ton mile. Considerable fluctuations in revenue were often caused by floods and periods of drought. The five-year averages, however, show that tolls and tonnage rose steadily:

Period	Average Annual Tolls (£)	Average Annual Tonnage
1795–1799	365	4,070
1800–1804	566	6,300
1805–1809	710	7,860
1810–1814	830	8,900
1815–1819	1,000	11,300

On only one occasion, before the opening of the Wey & Arun Junction Canal in 1816, was more than 10,000 tons carried in any one year, and William Smith, the wharfinger at Midhurst, stated in 1814 that the navigation 'has never paid an interest at all adequate to the expenditure in completing and keeping up the navigation'. But judged by what was earned on other agricultural waterways at the same period, the Rother was doing quite well; on a net expenditure of about £16,000 revenue receipts were giving a gross return rising from less than 2 per cent in 1798 to about 7 per cent in 1813. As soon as barges could reach the Thames, Lord Egremont mused, the traffic could substantially increase.

CHAPTER EIGHT

LOCAL DIFFICULTIES AND TROUBLESOME DISPUTES (1795–1819)

John Shean of Portsea – refusal to pay toll on timber – Jessop's opinion – jury award damages to Lord Egremont – meetings held to decide on the appointment of a land valuer (1795) – George Smallpiece – attitudes of owners and occupiers – wastage of water at Stopham Lock – troublesome people – the Hollist affair (1807–9) – the Egremont v. Stoveld dispute (1814–18) – William Stoveld – claims that timber should be charged by measure and not by weight – refuses to pay tolls – Lord Egremont sues for non-payment and wins – definition of square timber – first action heard at Horsham – second hearing at Lewes – Lord Egremont petitions House of Commons to have the Rother Navigation Act amended (1816) – bill withdrawn – the bailiff of Midhurst petitions Lord Egremont to maintain the navigation – Stoveld's final ruse – Lord Egremont requires all barges to have two indexes – Stoveld's complaint against King (1819) – drainage problems – Charles Biddulph and a faulty culvert (1819) – the case of Blanch v. Jarrett – liability for harbour dues on chalk contested by Lord Egremont.

The collection of unpaid accounts was providing a problem even before the navigation was completed. The normal practice was for bargemasters to pay their dues to the collector at Fittleworth Lock. However, in cases where a number of barges belonged to or were engaged by one principal, quarterly accounts were made up and rendered by Thomas Upton. It was the dilatoriness of payment by some of the latter which prompted his lordship to issue a stern warning. In the case of John Shean, a builder from Portsea, this warning was completely ignored. Shean owed £85 3s 2¾d for tolls and wharfage due on forty-nine cargoes from Coultershaw and Lodsbridge between August 1793 and September 1794. When James Upton Tripp wrote to him in October demanding immediate payment, Shean replied that he had 'no objection to paying the legal demand'. What he did object to was the way the toll was charged on timber, but it was not until 9 January 1795 that he wrote to Lord Egremont on this point. By this time he had been 'indebted' at Petworth. Shean argued that his cargoes of rails and tub staves, being scantling 2½ inches thick and 4 to 6 inches wide, should be charged by weight and not by measure. 'I have always computed it at 600 feet run to make 60 square feet . . . and have found the bargemen, carriers and masters of vessels very ready to carry it in preference to timber or plank.' Shean went on to suggest that the action for unpaid tolls commenced by his lordship's solicitor should be settled by arbitration.

Egremont sought William Jessop's advice. Jessop replied in February that plank specifically designated as plank in the Act could not be classed as timber. However, he added; 'I apprehend that except for the inconvenience that will attend the measuring of small pieces, it would be in his lordship's interest to be paid by measure rather than by weight.' Jessop pointed out that the number of feet to a ton of wood varied considerably. Oak was normally assessed at 39 feet compared with beech 42, ash 45, maple 48, walnut 57, and elm and fir 60. If, however, the wood was green or soaked in water they would weigh more. It is significant that Jessop's figures were at variance with those specified in the Act (Section XVIII) which laid down 40 feet for oak, ash and elm and 50 feet for fir, deal, poplar and other wood. Consequently timber merchants were being asked to pay a higher toll rate on woods like elm and fir than would normally have been demanded on other navigations, but less for oak, maple and particularly beech.[83]

Lord Egremont sued for £200 damages. Shean offered to pay £64 14s 7d into court after computing his debt at 500 feet to 50 square feet 'to avoid doubt about the quantity'. As was laid down by the Act the under-sheriff thereupon summoned a jury to the Half Moon Inn at Petworth in April to testify the facts before the case was heard in the Court of Common Pleas. Yet the case never came to trial as Shean thought 'the matter in dispute not of consequence sufficient to engage a contest at the assizes' and he finally paid his lordship's bill for damages and costs on 6 May 1795. However, the method used to calculate the toll on timber carried on the navigation continued to give rise to great dissatisfaction.

It was not until 30 April 1795 that James Upton Tripp wrote to all the owners and occupiers of land taken or damaged by the 'completion' of the navigation to announce, with little advance warning, that on Thursday 7 May a meeting would be held at the Spread Eagle in Midhurst to 'fix on a proper person' to carry out the valuation. A similar meeting was arranged for two days later at the Half Moon in Petworth.

Some of those who could not attend either meeting wrote to Mr Tripp. William Fuller of Storrington considered the area of his piece of land 'so trifling' that he would be content to go along with whatever the meeting decided. Mr Jones wrote from Chelsea that 'the general tenor of Lord Egremont's character puts him beyond suspicion that he would wish to take advantage of any man. I for my part wish for no more than is equitable.' Mr Johnson being in town (London) had only just received his invitation and found it impossible to attend 'tomorrow's meeting'. The Earl of Newburgh, who lived at Slindon House, was invited to attend, but, as his agent pointed out, his lands were not in fact injured by the navigation. Thirty people attended the Midhurst meeting and twenty-seven that held at Petworth.

Five surveyors were considered for the post. One of them, John Ewon of Abinger, thought two valuers and not one should be selected as 'even then it is ten to one if all parties are satisfied'. He recommended Smallpiece of Stoke and Ewon of Petersfield as being 'most in practice', and mentioned that no surveyor in this country goes out upon such business for under two guineas a day and their expenses and that they seldom went out by the day on such jobs as this. In spite of these reservations he was willing to let his name go forward. He was not selected. The injured parties picked George Smallpiece in favour of Ewon, Chilton of Cuckfield and Eager of Cranleigh.

Smallpiece began his valuation in August 1795, riding round the neighbourhood and spending five and a half days getting in and out of William Duff's boat. It was soon found that there was a general lack of information about whose land was what; consequently Duff had to spend a week in September helping Thomas Upton measure the land cut away; in this Upton was assisted by numerous people who were given beer for their help in delineating the boundaries. By now the season was too advanced for any further valuations to be carried out and so the work was postponed until the following May when Duff again ferried Smallpiece, with his two assistants, up and down the navigation and shared the largesse of beer, cider, bread and cheese which over two days cost his lordship 10s 3½d.

Smallpiece's correspondence with Tripp reveals that compensation to occupiers of land was based solely on the annual rental per acre, but that damage to property was separately assessed. A field beside Cowdray Park, occupied by Mr Capron, was rated at 22s per acre, a meadow nearby at 30s per acre.

The great advantage of land transport over water is that in the event of a road or railway becoming blocked there is usually no great difficulty in finding an alternative route. With most canal and river navigations, however, there were few alternatives. It was usually floods rather than drought or ice which caused the major stoppages of traffic. The Arun Valley was renowned for its flooding at almost any time of the year and the same applied to a rather lesser extent to the Rother Valley. Once the waters rose 5 ft or so above normal, even barges only half full could not pass beneath the bridges. Traffic in fact was usually halted for twenty to thirty days a year and sometimes more.

The navigation took great pains to preserve its water supply and was empowered to prosecute those who deliberately wasted it. In dry seasons a barge going down was expected to wait for a barge coming up if it was within

200 yards of the lock, at which distance the Act stipulated that a guide-post had to be erected to indicate the point. The 1791 Act designated a fine of £2 to £5 if the cloughs of the upper gates were drawn before the lower gates were closed.

There was rarely a winter when the floods did not swirl around Stopham House, so it was not perhaps surprising that Walter Smyth should not be overconcerned if the paddles of Stopham Lock were left open to allow water to flow through the lock. This laxity came to the notice of Lord Egremont, who was forced in 1801 to write a personal note to Smyth – better, he thought, if he wrote himself rather than ask Mr Upton – to explain the importance of not allowing water to run through the locks. Egremont then went on to relate how he had advertised a reward of three guineas the previous year to anyone informing against a person drawing the cloughs of the locks.★ When an informer had advised him that the miscreant was none other than one of Mr Smyth's servants, Egremont declined to prosecute to 'avoid everything which might possibly be construed as unpleasant'. However, he could not refrain from pointing out that he had still paid the informer three guineas as 'it would have been very unjust for him to have been a loser on account of my delicacy towards you' (Mr Smyth). Egremont also announced that he was intending to advertise a new reward and to prosecute in future. 'I thought it best to inform you of it first and to send you a copy of the advertisement I intend to put up.'†84 This tactful letter presumably had the desired effect.

Over the years land ownership has probably been the source of more minor disputes and of more fees to the legal profession than any other. Although Lord Egremont owned or purchased‡ the freehold of much of the land needed for the navigation, there were still a number of landowners who discovered either that the navigation had severed their access to a strip of land or had created some sort of potential nuisance like a faulty culvert. In July 1807 Lord Egremont attempted to resolve such a dispute over the ownership of a piece of meadow measuring less than half an acre (1 rod and 19 perches to be precise).

The land in question was part of East Common meadow, which was cut off

★ Upton's accounts show payments of £3 3s for informing against Francis Jarrett for leaving the lower lock at Haslingbourne in an improper manner (May 1798) and against J. Herrington for drawing up and leaving so the cloughs of Stopham lock-gates (June 1800).

† In June 1801 notices were posted along the navigation stating that persons giving information leading to the conviction of offenders would be rewarded.

‡ A note dated 30 October 1796 (PHA F13/16a) proposes that Lord Egremont should exchange with Mr Poyntz some 15 acres of land by Cowdray Park valued at £548.

from the Lodsworth part of the meadow by the lock cut made in 1793. The valuer George Smallpiece had directed that it should be purchased by Lord Egremont from George Caplin and John Reid. It appears that a Mr Hollist contracted to purchase Reid's moiety about April 1799 and the former claimed to have done so on the grounds that Reid had a defective title to sell to Lord Egremont, 'which defect', wrote his lordship's attorney, 'has never been well understood'.

Hollist, a barrister of Pump Court in the Temple, whose family seat was Lodsworth House, challenged Egremont's right to the meadow in a letter dated 22 June 1807: 'on a subject, tho' of small moment, of which I received information . . . that last week some workmen of Your Lordship's cut the grass of a small piece of meadow (I believe in East Mead . . .) and carried the hay away, an act as I conceive not consistent with law'.

On 4 July Lord Egremont took the trouble to call personally on Hollist, but the latter's 'imperfectly established state of health' necessarily induced him to leave chambers between three and four o'clock so that his lordship could but leave a note. Hollist wrote a long letter in reply on Sunday stating his claim and concluded: 'I have availed myself of this leisure day to write this.' A further letter from Hollist written on 22 July told how he had written to Mr Capron, one of the valuers, regarding Mr Barlow's measurements taken in 1796. As Hollist had only one servant in town he begged his lordship to excuse him sending his letter by post.

Twelve days later Hollist wrote to Lord Egremont saying that after perusing the Act he fancied that as the value of the land was not set by the commissioners but by Mr Smallpiece, and that consequently if the owners did not appear before the commissioners no adjudication by them would be valid. As Hollist had hoped to have 'accidentally met' his lordship in town or been able to see him at Petworth but had not done so, he wrote again in June 1808 to say that 'being perfectly satisfied of my right to the little piece of meadow land' he has instructed his tenant to cut the grass; he pointed out that 'your people having cut and taken the grass last year after he had told the Earl's servants that he (Egremont) would be liable for an action to trespass if they did', and that 'I flatter myself that your lordship will think it but just that Barnes, his tenant, should be paid for his last year's grass', since 'he is a very honest, industrious man and has I believe a large family'.

This letter produced a quick response from Lord Egremont proposing to let Hollist have the land to which the latter tartly replied that the land was already his and that he expected his lordship to admit he was in the wrong.

Apparently Hollist claimed that Lord Egremont had paid Reid for the land instead of Tribe's executors who had sold the land to Hollist. Hollist had a legal conveyance to the land and Lord Egremont had none.

Both parties submitted this dispute to an arbitrator, Mr Mitford, who some twelve months later was forced to concede failure. Writing to Tyler he had to 'lament that his wish to collect information which might have tended towards enabling a settlement has entirely failed'.[85]

There were heavy snowfalls in the winter of 1813 and the thaw was followed by a great flood which washed away part of the tow-path beneath Shopham Bridge and undermined the buttress of the central pier which collapsed about mid-summer. To save the bridge collapsing, Thomas Upton had to arrange for twenty or more loads of heavy stone to be placed around the pier and for the small island upstream of the bridge to be removed to allow the water a freer passage through the centre arch.

In 1814 there finally erupted what had been a vexatious disagreement between Lord Egremont and William Stoveld over the method to be adopted in assessing the dues to be levied on timber and plank. It was an extraordinary dispute because whichever way the toll was calculated the difference in toll was usually negligible.★ Yet at one time it seemed that the earl would close the navigation rather than be worsted.

Stoveld (1766–1841) was a well-known Petworth timber and coal merchant besides being the owner and part-owner of several barges using the navigation.† The principal point in dispute was whether the tolls and wharfage charges on timber should be calculated by measure or by weight. The Act of Parliament laid down that since timber was difficult to weigh due to its size, 'for the better ascertaining the tonnage of timber and wood' it was agreed that 26 feet of round or 40 feet of square hewn oak, ash or elm or 50 feet of fir, deal, poplar or other wood should be rated as one ton.

The dispute came to public notice in May 1814 when a letter signed by Stoveld and others using the navigation stated that they felt aggrieved by being erroneously charged for timber by weight instead of by measure and that they would henceforth refuse to pay tolls and wharfage dues calculated in this manner. Egremont's lawyers, however, believed that not only did the Act

---

★ Thirty barge-loads of oak carried in 1816–17 were both measured and weighed. In fourteen instances measured tons were greater than weighed, in two they were the same and in the other fourteen weighed tonnage was greater. The difference between measured ($598\frac{1}{2}$) and weighed ($600\frac{1}{4}$) tonnage for the thirty loads was a mere $1\frac{3}{4}$ tons (PHA O.F. 13/166).

† In 1798 William Stoveld lived at Whithurst, Kirdford. This was a 96-acre farm which had a few cattle, thirty-one sheep, two pigs, six carts and wagons and harvested both wheat and oats (*Sussex Archaeological Collections 1950*, vol. LXXXIX, p. 71). It was timber, however, in which he began to successfully speculate. Records show that he bought considerable stocks at various times. In 1817 he paid the Leggatt family £1,730 for timber in the Kirdford, Billingshurst and Wisborough Green area. It also appears that Stoveld acted as a timber agent for the government (ms. Stoveld to William Tyler, 6 March 1819).

clearly set out how the lengths of timber should be converted into tons, but that Stoveld and his fellow merchants had acquiesced in paying tolls by weight since they had done so since the opening of the navigation. Indeed, William Jessop had advised Lord Egremont on the subject some twenty years before at the time of the Shean dispute:

> Plank is distinguished by name from timber in the Act – and as every one knows – that fir plank – commonly called deals – is never called timber – it is fairly to be presumed to be the intention of the Act, and it is consonant to the common acceptation of the word – that timber means the body of tree either round as it is fallen or only squared by taking off the limbs to lighten the weight of carriage and that it is not called timber when cut into planks – scantling, or small pieces and the words 'for better ascertaining' clearly shows this to be the meaning of the Act – because a tree being too unmanageable to weigh is best ascertained by measuring – but small pieces which it would be very troublesome to measure are best ascertained by weight.

The plaintiffs' case was based on the fact that it was common practice on most navigations to calculate tolls on timber by measure which they claimed raised a lower charge than if calculated by weight.

The first round of the dispute was straightforward enough. Lord Egremont sued Stoveld for non-payment of tolls. The case was heard in the King's Bench Division in the Strand on 7 November 1814. John King, the collector of tolls and lock-keeper at Fittleworth, gave evidence stating that all the barges coming up and down the navigation were weighed by gauge at Fittleworth and charged accordingly. The court found for Lord Egremont and awarded him £81 5s of the £85 10s 11d claimed to be due.

Stoveld now sought to establish that the relevant section of the Rother Navigation Act should be construed to allow timber, wood and plank to be charged by measure. At the hearing at the Sussex Lent Assizes in Horsham on 20 March 1815, before Mr Baron Wood, the definition of what constituted square timber was hotly debated. At length the jury agreed that scantlings, thick stuff and plank could be called square timber and found for Lord Egremont who was awarded £1,000 damages and 40s costs. Unfortunately this verdict left it unclear as to whether the calculation of the toll on timber by measure should be confined to the body of the tree hewn square or to include planks and other articles into which the body of the tree had been converted. It was therefore agreed to hold a fresh trial. This took place at the Summer Assizes in Lewes when the jury 'having found that the payment by measure was confined to round timber and that which was hewn square, the

Court again entered a verdict for the plaintiff of £1,000 damages and 40s costs'.

The Lewes award was nevertheless subject to arbitration before William Bollard of the Inner Temple to ascertain the exact amount of damages. Counsel's opinion was sought. Samuel Marryat averred (16 July 1815) that it could be argued that timber tolls by measure might not apply when calculating wharfage charges 'though the question is one of nicety'. Until a few days before the hearing on 18 and 19 January 1816 it had been accepted by both parties that Mr Bollard was only to consider the sole point in dispute, in other words whether square hewn timber should be paid for by measure or by weight. However, at the last moment Stoveld entered an objection to paying for all articles charged by weight according to the indices of the barges containing such cargo. In fact Stoveld argued that the referee should reconsider the verdict itself and the cost of the action.

The earl's initial reaction to the Lewes decision was one of fury. Indeed so disenchanted had his lordship become with the tiresome dispute with the timber merchant that he seriously considered abandoning the navigation. Already he had allowed the state of the navigation to deteriorate. In May 1815 John Challen reported to Tyler that a bargeman, Stephen Hurst (who worked for Thomas Isemonger, the Littlehampton shipbuilder) had reported that both Shopham and Todham Locks were 'greatly at fault' and that the shoals at Coultershaw and Todham prevented him getting up to Midhurst. Tyler curtly replied that he didn't manage the navigation but 'he would tell my lord of it'. In July Egremont sought counsel's opinion as to whether he had to maintain the Rother in a navigable state and was advised by Samuel Marryat that he did not have to do so and was 'quite at liberty to discontinue the employment of the ballast barge' whenever he thought fit. In the meantime his lawyers prepared a bill for an Act to amend 'the vexatious clause'. The petition for this bill was brought to the House of Lords in February 1816 on the grounds that 'whereas the computation of tolls by measure instead of by weight denoted by the index had been found by experience to be "difficult, uncertain and inconvenient" it was expedient that the clause relating to measure should be changed'. On 22 February leave was granted and the bill had its first reading on 15 March. But then something happened which caused Egremont to decide, at a time when the Wey & Arun Junction Canal was nearing completion, to drop the matter. At the same time he appears to have taken the dramatic decision to cease maintaining the navigation.

What actually occurred can only be surmised but it is probable that his legal advisers had intimated that Lord Egremont might not get the Act he wanted. It has to be appreciated that the whole system of weights and measures in England at that time was confusing. Young gives examples of several types of acres (short, statute, forest, etc.) of different sizes; how a load of wheat was 40 bushels but of oats 80 bushels and how both troy and avoirdupois were in use.[86] But it was perhaps the realization of the type of individual he was dealing with which made Egremont act as he did.

Little vexations continued. In September (1816) King wrote to Upton saying that one of Stoveld's bargemen had said that as his plank was very dirty, Mr Stoveld claimed he was to be allowed one ton for dirt otherwise he was not to take the barge through. Upton promptly replied: 'You must allow nothing for dirt but charge according to the index.'

However, more fraudulent action was afoot, although this was not discovered until 8 July 1817 when John King reported to Thomas Upton that he had noticed something curious when weighing Stoveld's barge no. 73. The index had shown only $10\frac{1}{2}$ tons when from past experience he knew it must be nearer 12. He had challenged the bargemaster George White, who had at once admitted that the index marks had been altered. White had at once offered to pay the toll on $12\frac{1}{2}$ tons but King informed Upton who had the barge weighed at Rotherbridge later that day and found the actual weight to be $13\frac{3}{4}$ tons. Apparently the previous autumn (1816) Samuel Winter, a barge builder, had been asked by Thomas Overington, Stoveld's agent, to alter the indices on some five or six barges owned or partly owned by Stoveld. Lord Egremont was angrier than ever. There was, he thought, no point in prosecuting White, who was but a pawn in the matter and a poor man into the bargain, but he would have Stoveld for fraud.

Depositions against the timber merchant were at once lodged before the local justices. However, Lord Egremont's attorneys were a little concerned since Stoveld could claim that Lord Egremont had failed to implement certain of the Act's requirements. For instance, no milestones had been erected to indicate distances nor had by-laws been introduced describing how the indexes that were wrong should be displayed.★ Stoveld also felt that he should have been warned that his indexes were wrong before being prosecuted; but apparently when Upton had asked him to correct his indices he had refused unless Lord Egremont paid half the cost.

Meanwhile the navigation began to deteriorate to such an extent that in the summer of 1816 the bailiff and burgesses of Midhurst and some 120 inhabitants were forced to petition his lordship to maintain the navigation, claiming that the river near the town was in so bad a state due to shoals of

---

★   The Act directed that two indexes should be placed on each side of every barge and not as had become the custom at the head and stern of each barge.

sand 'as to render it absolutely necessary to load and unload the barges on private property'. So serious was the problem that a total stoppage of trade was predicted.

Lord Egremont was persuaded to reconsider his position and in due course maintenance was resumed. In November 1817 James Monk the bailiff was able to write and thank the earl for 'this mark of Your Lordship's favour towards' the inhabitants of the town and neighbourhood of Midhurst. At length, in July 1818 Lord Egremont had notices printed and circulated stating that two indexes should be fixed on each side of every barge with effect from 1 September 1818.

One of Lord Egremont's particular interests was how best to drain his water meadows. Arthur Young describes how this was attempted, records some of his failures and noted that 'this operation is not yet thoroughly understood'. Egremont engaged various individuals including a Mr Elkington, who claimed a wide knowledge and experience in draining boggy land. However, nearly all of Elkington's efforts at Petworth failed, including the attempted draining of Budham meadow which lay above Rotherbridge Farm. After digging a new drain 200 yards long at the expense of £100, he found the meadow was flooded by springs from higher ground when the ditch was stopped up and by the river when the ditch was left open. Elkington thereupon suggested embanking the river and building a windmill to pump the ditch dry. Lord Egremont decided to try another method. Discovering that the meadows on the opposite side to Budham were lower, he had a wooden trunk laid across the bed of the river which was carried by an open drain through the meadows and by means of a pipe under the turnpike at Rotherbridge to join the river below Coultershaw Mill.

During the spring of 1819 a protracted correspondence began between his lordship's attorney and Charles Biddulph★ of Burton Park concerning another drainage problem. The facts were simple enough: a faulty culvert near Shopham Lock had caused some 4 acres of meadowland to be regularly flooded; but Lord Egremont's offer to remedy the nuisance by putting in a new drain was qualified by the condition that he would not be liable for its future repair. Biddulph would only agree subject to 'the work being found to answer the purpose effectually'. Such a reply did not amuse his lordship and Biddulph was compelled to explain that as soon as Thomas Upton had rebuilt the drain and this had been found to answer the purpose by a trial of its effect after the first flood, he would undertake to maintain the drain. A third letter in April stated that Biddulph had 'the highest opinion of Lord Egremont's

★ Died a bachelor in 1821.

Rother Navigation.

IN Pursuance and under the Authority of the Act of Parliament, for making and maintaining the River Rother navigable, and for other Purposes; I, George Obrien EARL of EGREMONT, do hereby direct and appoint, that, on all Boats Barges or other Vessels, passing on the River Rother Navigation, or on any Part thereof, TWO INDEXES, of Copper Lead or other Metal, of graduated Figures, denoting the Weight or Tonnage of the Lading, shall be fixed *on each Side* of every such Boat Barge or other Vessel; and that one of the said Indexes shall be fixed on or near to the Stem Post on one Side of each such Boat Barge or other Vessel, and another of the said Indexes shall be fixed on or near to the Stern Post on the other Side of such Boat Barge or other Vessel; and that one other of the said Indexes shall be fixed on or near to the middle of each Side of every such Boat Barge or other Vessel; so as that the Distance between the two Indexes on each Side shall be (as nearly as may be) one half of the whole Length of the Boat Barge or other Vessel; and so that the true Weight of the Lading of every such Boat Barge or other Vessel may at all times clearly appear. And I do hereby give Notice, that every Owner Master or other Person having the Command of any Boat Barge or other Vessel, which shall, from and after the FIRST Day of SEPTEMBER next, pass on the said Navigation or any Part thereof, without having such Indexes fixed as aforesaid, so that the true Weight of the Lading of such Boat Barge or other Vessel may at all times clearly appear, will be proceeded against for Recovery of the Penalty by the Act imposed for such Default. Dated this Twentieth Day of July 1818.

Egremont.

Lord Egremont's belated notice to bargemasters, issued in July 1818 but which should have been circulated in accordance with the Act when the navigation was opened.

judgement as a man and a very high opinion of Mr Upton's talent as an engineer, but I do not believe in the infallibility of either'.

The meadow in question lay upstream of the lock and was lower than the banks of the river; the proposed remedy was complicated by the fact that in order to carry out the work it would be necessary to dig a drain through land owned by neighbours who cared not a jot whether Biddulph's meadow was flooded or not. His lordship also feared the possibility of the works failing on their first trial due to possible neglect in not keeping the drain properly open. The correspondence grew more bitter. In his fifth letter Biddulph was provoked into commenting on his lordship's view 'that he never saw such a proposal as mine in all his life', by having to confess that 'as his health was not as to admit of continuing single-handed a protracted correspondence', the matter be best referred to Messrs Holmes, his solicitors in Arundel.

The problems appeared to have all been settled when, on 5 May, Biddulph advised Tyler that circumstances had arisen which prevented him signing the undertaking. What these circumstances were was not explained. Thus, as consent for Egremont's proposal was not forthcoming, the only alternative was the expensive one of building a new culvert under the river. In September it is recorded that the problem was resolved by 'sinking the old wood culvert deeper under the river between Mr Biddulph's meadow and Wide Meadow and altering the brick ends to the culvert'.

An attempt was made in 1819 by the commissioners of the Port of Arundel to levy harbour dues on chalk exported coastwise through Littlehampton. John Strudwick, a bargeman from Pulborough, gave evidence that in all his forty years on the river the chalk ballast removed from vessels at Littlehampton and sold to farmers for manure had never been subject to duty. However, in December John Blanch, the tide surveyor of the Port of Arundel, demanded £6 10s 9d duty from Francis Jarrett, the manager of the Houghton Chalk Pits whose sloop *Hero* had been stopped from going to sea, the main sail removed and the vessel put in dock because the master had refused to pay the duty.

Jarrett resisted the commissioners' demands because no previous request for payment had been made since the establishment of the chalk works at Amberley nearly twenty years before. The commissioners intimated that they were willing to place the question 'in any mode of trying the right that may be least expensive and least incumbered with technical terms and difficulties'. Counsel's opinion on the case was that the commissioners had the right to raise a toll on every species of merchandise entering or leaving the port. The principal difficulty was to ascertain the toll rate, as chalk was not specified in the 1732 Littlehampton Harbour Act. The matter appears to have been left undecided until 1825 when a new Littlehampton Harbour Act included chalk in the schedule of goods, whether imported or exported, on which duties could be levied.

CHAPTER NINE

THE THAMES TRADE (1816–71)

The completion of the Petworth Canal had been a tentative initiative towards building a navigation to link the Thames and the English Channel. However, plans for extending it had had to be discarded on the grounds of impracticability. Efforts to extend the Arun Canal, too, had been initially frustrated by the failure to obtain either the approval of the Wey Navigation or Arun Navigation proprietors. Further attempts to obtain agreement were postponed as a consequence of the war with France. The resultant economic depression had also ensured that none of the schemes mooted at the beginning of the nineteenth century to link London and the English Channel came to fruition.

In 1799 William Jessop had prepared a scheme for a horse railway from Wandsworth. Nothing came of this idea but completion of the Surrey Iron Railway to Croydon in 1803 gave further impetus to proposals to extend it to Reigate and the south coast. John Rennie designed a 100-mile waterway from the terminus of the Croydon Canal to Portsmouth which envisaged forty-one locks and a 4½-mile tunnel. In 1807 it was hoped to link either the Basingstoke Canal or the Wey Navigation to the Itchen at Winchester by building a 35-mile barge canal with a 2-mile long tunnel between Alresford and Alton. In 1810 Rennie published the prospectus for the Grand Southern Canal – an ambitious 95-mile scheme to link the Medway at Tonbridge to Portsmouth. Although subscriptions of £650,000 were promised, the parliamentary bill was lost on the second reading by 100 votes to 17.

Although these ideas came to nothing they were the cause of delaying Lord Egremont's own venture. His plan to extend the Arun Canal from Newbridge to Shalford finally got underway in the autumn of 1811, when on Saturday 1 June 1811 he personally launched the public appeal at the White Hart Inn in Guildford. The prospectus of the proposed Wey & Arun Junction Canal was redrafted by his lordship before it appeared in *The Times* on 17 October 1811. A full account of how the Act of Parliament was obtained in 1813, and the canal built and opened, is given in *London's Lost Route to the Sea* (David & Charles, 4th edition, 1986).

The official opening of the Wey & Arun Junction Canal took place on 29 September 1816. Four gaily decorated barges carried the Earl of Egremont and over a hundred guests from Alfold to Guildford. Two bands entertained the gathering, while a string of eight barges, laden with coal and stacked with timber, followed in their wake. William Upton from Petworth represented the Rother Navigation's commercial interest in his new lighter, or passage boat, as it is variously described.

The opening of the Wey & Arun Junction Canal provided the towns and villages along the Rother Navigation with water communication not only to Guildford, Godalming and London, but to the network of inland waterways which stretched from the Thames to Bristol, Liverpool and the industrial cities of the north. It is likely that the significance of this facility to the townspeople of Midhurst was only dimly perceived, but Lord Egremont had realized his cherished ambition of linking Petworth to the Thames.

However, the amount of traffic generated by the opening of the canal was disappointingly small. Because traffic was slow to develop on the Wey & Arun Junction Canal, much consideration was given to the question of toll reductions. The Wey Navigation had reduced its rates on coal after the opening of the canal so that Guildford and Godalming continued to rely on the Wey for their coal supplies. Even village merchants along the northern sector of the canal at Bramley, Cranleigh, Loxwood and beyond were using the Wey to the detriment of the Arun Navigation. In an attempt to redress the balance, both the Arun and the Wey & Arun Navigations reduced their toll on coal in 1819. The reason was principally because the traffic wasn't there to be had. The end of the Napoleonic Wars had removed the strongest motive for merchants to consider sending goods and materials by inland waterway from London to Littlehampton. The ever-present risk of shipwreck in the Dover Straits did not justify the greater hazards of delay and pilferage and the greater expense arising from payment of tolls to each of six different navigation concerns (Thames, Wey, Godalming, Wey & Arun, Arun, Port of Arundel) and the cost of transhipment to Portsmouth. It was stated in 1817 that the 2,500 tons of goods carried between Arundel and Portsmouth had to be transhipped at Arundel from barges into sea-going vessels 'which are often delayed in Arundel river for several weeks if the wind sets on the shore'.

Another reason was the lack of promotion. Although toll concessions on goods passing through the new canal had been incorporated in the Act of Parliament, no similar concessions had so far been introduced by the existing navigations; nor, indeed, by the Rother. In May 1817 Thomas Upton rather belatedly wrote to John King that Lord Egremont had agreed to reduce the toll by one third on all goods brought from the Wey Navigation up the Rother to Haslingbourne or Coultershaw or above (but not below) and for 'all the new trade going down from these points (or from above) through the Wey & Arun Junction Canal into the Wey'. The lower rate was not to include bark, timber nor any of its conversions since they already went down the Rother into the Arun. This exception evidently mitigated against good business, for two months later Upton is again writing to King: 'It has been explained to me, and I am satisfied, that bark and spokes carried by this new lighter down the Rother . . . to London is a new trade and, if loaded at Coultershaw and Haslingbourne or above, should be charged two pence instead of three pence a ton mile.' However, such reduction was still not to apply to such items being carried to Littlehampton. (What is not clear is why traffic to points below Petworth was not also granted this concession nor whether the concession applied to barges as well as lighters.)

In some ways the navigation was run on a very casual footing; that was Lord Egremont's style. Not until after the opening of the Wey & Arun Junction Canal did he arrange for any rents to be collected for the wharf buildings erected at Fittleworth, Coultershaw and Midhurst. In 1818 Henry and William Upton were licensed to build coal pens at Coultershaw, but rents, although backdated, were not collected until 1821. His lordship clearly wished to promote trade by charging modest annual rates, 2s 6d for a coal pen, 5s for a warehouse. Total rents receivable between 1818 and 1846 never exceeded £3 per annum.

Traffic at Coultershaw continued to develop. In 1820, 1,683 tons of coal had been deposited there. To improve efficiency Thomas Overington, the under-wharfinger, was told to look after the mill meadow and check all traffic. He was paid 2d a time for listing 619 barges that year. In 1824 James Tribe took over this responsibility. The market town of Petworth (whose population had risen from 2,264 in 1801 to 2,781 in 1821) and the surrounding farmsteads now looked to Coultershaw for the arrival of their coal and groceries; for their fertilizers and fancy goods from London, Guildford and Arundel; and as the most convenient means of dispatching timber, their own wares and farm produce to market.

John King's successor at Fittleworth Wharf was an unrelated namesake, a single man, aged forty-nine, who was formerly a bricklayer. He lived in a small cottage adjoining Fittleworth Common in the Bishop's Manor; it had a blacksmith's shop and a large garden of about one acre. King also had a little business at the 'stone pits at Pulborough', which he ran for Mr Sandham of Horsham; this brought him £8 or £10 p.a. and took up half a day once a fortnight besides the paperwork which he did at home. John King II looked after the navigation from Shopham Bridge to the Arun for twenty years until he died in October 1840.

The characters working the navigation do not appear to have been a very lovable lot. Of the petty mindedness of John King I, the lock-keeper at Fittleworth, we have already commented in Chapter Seven. The wharfinger at Midhurst, however, appears to have been decidedly disagreeable. William Goodner succeeded William Smith in 1820 on the recommendation of Mr Stoveld 'who had a great deal to do at Midhurst Wharf at the time'. Goodner spent twelve years there but Thomas Upton, among others, found fault with him for quarrelling; he was also careless in keeping records of the timber brought up by water and removed from the wharf by land, which cumulated in the Biffin dispute of 1828 when the merchant was only charged for twenty-five loads instead of fifty. As a consequence Goodner was sacked in June 1830 and John Smart appointed on the same terms; in other words he was paid 3d a ton for stacking timber and plank. At the other wharves it was customary for the merchants to employ and pay the wharfingers.[87]

In January 1819 there was still some confusion over the toll rates. King reported to Upton that Stoveld was offering to send all his goods via the Wey & Arun at 2d a ton 'but now finds 3d a ton is again charged'. King asked if this was a mistake 'as 2d a ton is the same the lighters pay'.

The main stumbling block to the development of trade was the different toll rates for each navigation. To reach London from Petworth tolls had to be paid not only to the Rother Navigation, but to the Arun, the Wey & Arun, the Godalming, the Wey and the Thames navigations. Some reduction in the rates charged on through traffic had been negotiated, for example for traffic passing through the Wey & Arun but not from the Rother. Consequently several merchants and bargemasters drew the attention of Lord Egremont to this anomaly, but possibly because William Stoveld was the chief trader on the Rother, little was done. Stoveld attended a meeting of the Wey & Arun Canal Company at Guildford in February 1819 at which the company agreed to reduce the toll on timber and hoops to that of coal. In a letter to William Tyler dated 6 March 1819, Stoveld wrote that he had 'a great deal of timber in the neighbourhood of

COALS

Retailing at Richard Isemonger's

NEW DEAL, TIMBER & COAL WHARF,

AT LITTLEHAMPTON.

At   per Chaldron.

Barge Chichester to

Midhurst — Aug 9 1822

22 tons

Isemonger & Son's barges left from Chichester and Littlehampton two or three times a week bound for Three Cranes Wharf by Southwark Bridge. In the late autumn of 1822 George Collier, master of Richard Isemonger's lighter, dropped his winch in Coultershaw Lock and took the navigation. Isemonger had to pay 6s 4½d to replace it.

Fernhurst, Lynchmere, Trotton, Rogate and Wardley Marsh' and that unless the Rother reduced its toll on timber from 3*d* to 2*d* a ton mile for barges as it had for lighters, he would send his goods coastways as the difference was 1*s* 6*d* per load. It seems that this reduction may have been agreed. Before 1820 the Wey ledgers record only three cargoes from the Rother proceeding beyond Guildford. In 1817 Stoveld had taken 20 tons of timber to Pyrford and 20 tons to Newark, and in 1819, 26¼ tons to London. Not until the summer of 1820 did Stoveld make frequent trips to Godalming, taking 253½ tons of timber to Marshall's yard, and only in 1821 did he regularly carry timber, bark and charcoal to the Thames.

Although William Upton and Thomas Isemonger made odd voyages between Petworth and London, the only regular traffic between the Thames and Littlehampton was operated by Seward & Co. of Arundel. Their three barges *Arun, Commerce* and *Swallow* operated weekly, and sometimes thrice a fortnight, but they seldom carried loads of more than 20 or 25 tons. However, by 1823 an amalgamation had taken place and Seward, Henly & Co. had increased the size of their fleet to ten barges. The improvements carried out to the Arun Navigation in preparation for the opening of the Portsmouth & Arundel Canal enabled cargoes to be increased to 40 tons and over, and later that year, after the opening of the canal, the company was renamed the Portsmouth Barge Company.

On completion of the Wey & Arun Junction Canal, Lord Egremont had readily given his support to the building of the Portsmouth & Arundel Canal, whose Act had been passed in 1817. He was its largest shareholder, subscribing for 320 £50 shares which represented a little over $12\frac{1}{2}$ per cent of the company's capital. When the canal was opened in June 1823, his lordship led the pageant of eighteen boats from Ford in his gaily painted pleasure barge. At Hunston the procession was joined by an 80-ton schooner and five sloops before they 'moved majestically along with bands playing and colours flying towards Southgate Basin'. After spending the night at Chichester, Lord Egremont spent the following day voyaging through the Thorney and Langstone channels and the Portsea Canal to Portsmouth, where a further celebratory dinner was held. The completion of the waterway made possible direct inland water communication between London and Portsmouth, but had little bearing on the Rother Navigation traffic. Indeed, there is no record of any barge journeying between the Portsea Canal and Midhurst before the former canal ceased to function in 1825.

On 1 August 1823 William Cobbett spent the night at Petworth while on one of his rural rides. The following morning he set off towards Chichester and on reaching Coultershaw Wharf observed, as he had done at Newbridge the day before, that here too was 'another place of deposit for timber, lime, coals and other things'. At this time agricultural distress was at its worst but Cobbett could see no misery in this district and found fifty people haymaking in one of Lord Egremont's fields. Since the farmers had no employment for many of the men, one labourer was to be seen cracking the big stones laid in the road with a sledge-hammer.

The schemes being mooted for a ship canal from London to Portsmouth came to a climax in 1827. The most grandiose of these was Nicholas Cundy's plan for a Suez-size waterway to be called the Grand Imperial Ship Canal.★ It

---

★ q.v. *London's Lost Route to the Sea*, Chapter 9.

Coultershaw Flour Mill, *c.* 1905. The mill was burnt down in 1923, later rebuilt in ferroconcrete and subsequently demolished. This view is taken from the coal wharf on the north bank. The entrance to the lock is left of the picture.

Coultershaw Bridge and Lock, 1994. The lock chamber is in the background. It is surprising that this lock has survived since it has been threatened with destruction by the need to widen the narrow roadbridge carrying the A285 from Petworth to Chichester.

was to be 78 miles long from the Thames to Arundel and Portsmouth via Leatherhead and Newbridge, involving only eight locks and a 4-mile cutting over 130 ft deep between Dorking and Holmwood. It was proposed to cross the River Arun close to its junction with the River Rother at Stopham. John Rennie advised against the line, suggesting an alternative route via Guildford, Alford and Loxwood, and estimated the cost at a staggering £6½ million which caused interest in the project to be abandoned.

During the 1820s an odd assortment of cargoes appeared among the more mundane ledger entries of chalk, coal and timber. Powderwood (alder) used in the making of gunpowder, which accounted for over 70 tons in 1823, dropped substantially the following year and seemingly ceased to be carried again until many years later. Among the sundry cargoes of that decade were:

	tons
bacon	2
bottles (empty)	8¾
firewood	11½
glass	1
hurdles	1½
malt	20¼
mud	30
potatoes	8
rags	6½
reed	4
salt	55½
straw	1¾
turnips	26

Various items of furniture were sent down from London for Petworth House. Disappointingly, no details were given, only weights, for example 1¾ tons (1822), 1¾ tons (1823), 2¾ tons (1824), 2½ tons (1830), which leaves one to imagine whether the consignments were composed of choice antiques or statuary for Lord Egremont, or utility items for day-to-day use.

Efforts were made to identify the best means of making the navigation more profitable. In 1820, to avoid impositions by the bargemasters at Fittleworth, and possibly because the second John King was not able to exercise the same degree of control as his predecessor, Upton appointed Thomas Overington, the under-wharfinger at Coultershaw, to double-check the ladings with the toll tickets. Tuppence a boat was paid for this task.

Complaints about the high toll rates continued into the 1820s. In 1824 the Pulborough bargemaster William Warren drew Tyler's attention to the fact that local farmers were complaining about the price of chalk on the Rother and enquired whether his lordship intended reducing the toll. Warren claimed that the current rates made the sale of lime beyond Shopham Bridge uneconomical and that consequently his barges had only paid the trifling sum of about £6 in toll over the past three years. He pointed out that 14 tons of chalk and 1¼ tons of culm were required to fill each lime-kiln furnace which itself cost about sixpence and that if the toll was lowered to 1s a ton for the whole line, his lordship would not sustain any serious loss as 'there is a very considerable quantity of lime made use of as you approach Midhurst'. The average weight of a kiln of lime was 6 tons, and while this proposal seems reasonable no action was taken. Two years later Monk & Son of Midhurst suggested that traffic would greatly increase if the toll on all goods was reduced by a third. It was pointed out that whereas it cost about 2d a mile to carry coal from Stopham to Guildford, from Stopham to Midhurst it was nearer 4½d a mile.

Lord Egremont waited until 1828 before agreeing to reduce the toll on coal, timber and other items by a third to 2d a ton mile. As a result there was a 22 per cent increase in freight but a 12 per cent decrease in revenue.

In January 1833 Upton reported that the timber trade was 'very dull' and that there was a great deal of timber on Midhurst Wharf which had been there a year or more. 'I suppose the merchants cannot sell it.' Less easy to explain was the halving of the seaweed trade between 1830 and 1832. However, part of the loss in 1831 was made up by a trebling of the bog earth tonnage, and a 50 per cent increase in chalk traffic in 1832 suggests that either farmers may have preferred lime to seaweed as a fertilizer or that the seaweed was just not available.

The building and opening of the gasworks in 1836 on the southern outskirts of Petworth increased still further the number of horse-drawn carts hauling coal from the wharves at Coultershaw to the town.

Land and water carriage were in close competition in the 1830s for the transport of light goods and groceries. Boxall, the local carrier, travelled down from London to Petworth and Chichester every Friday in one third of the time it took for goods to arrive by water, but at considerably greater expense. To compete with land carriage fly barges were introduced which travelled day and night. Even so, the quickest journey from Queenhithe to Portsmouth was probably seldom quicker than that reported in the *Hampshire Telegraph* in June 1823 – 2 days 20 hours. Yet the main stumbling block remained the need for traders to calculate not only the cost of carriage but six different toll charges for estimating the charge for delivering goods from London to Petworth.

Some of the traffic was seasonal. Besides agricultural produce, hoops and spokes generally came down in the spring, oak bark in the autumn. There were also fluctuations caused by trade recessions. In 1832 the coal trade was up by 25 per cent, but that in timber, plank and bark fell by almost half.

It is indicative of the slow development of water carriage in southern England that even by the 1830s, the most prosperous decade of the canal age, there were no sizeable barge fleets on the navigations of Surrey, Sussex and Hampshire. The largest were those managed by the Arundel Lighter Co., John Birnie of Basingstoke and George Marshall of Godalming, but none of these operated more than twelve boats at any one time.

In 1830 the Wey registers showed that there were only five locally owned boats carrying cargoes from the Rother to the Thames. The pleasantly named *Albion, Algebra, Dart* and *Lark* all hailed from Fittleworth, and the *Sussex Oak* from Petworth. These five barges had four different owners. Thomas Barnard of Petworth exported timber to the Thames shipyards. The Fittleworth barges, run by William Strudwick and George and Joseph Smart, carried hoops to Godalming or Guildford and up the Wey. The tonnage carried was comparatively small. In 1830 only 365 tons left the Rother to be unloaded at wharves along the Wey and the Thames. The problem was picking up any return cargo. In 1830 they succeeded in obtaining only 38 tons. This, of course, was the problem for all bargemasters. Without regular back carriage, few could show a profit.

Traffic between the Rother Navigation, London and Chichester began to develop. Most barges were loaded and unloaded in the metropolis at the wharves south of Upper Thames Street. Queenhithe,* and the adjacent Three Cranes† and Bull wharves were advertised as ready to receive goods from Arundel and Chichester. Barges were loaded twice a week at Randell's Wharf, Queenhithe, while the Portsmouth & London fly barges departed Brook's Wharf every Saturday.

Pigot's Sussex trade directory of 1832 stated that Seward & Co.'s barges left from the canal basin at Chichester two or three times a week for Arundel, Petworth, Midhurst, and Randell's Wharf, Queenhithe, in the City of London. Samuel Tobitt was listed as the agent to the London, Arundel & Chichester Barge Company, High Street, Arundel, which was the principal carrier on the Arun, but its fleet did not use the Rother regularly until the 1820s by which time it had a fleet of ten barges. However, by the 1830s, when traffic on the navigation exceeded 12,000 or 13,000 tons a year, its

---

* A timber drawbridge, begun in 1426, allowed ships to pass through Old London Bridge to Queenhithe until London Bridge was rebuilt in the years 1824–31.

† Named after three strong timber cranes used for unloading wine on the Vintry Wharf. (John Stow Survey of London, 1598)

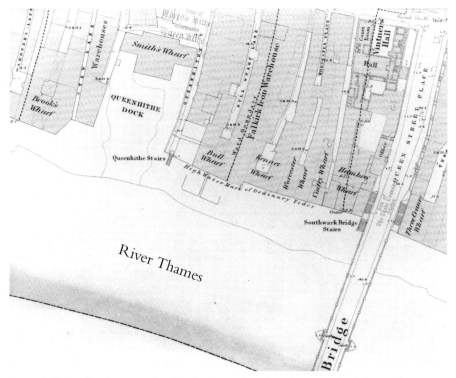

Queenhithe Dock, 1875. Merchandise for Petworth and Midhurst was loaded on to barges on the River Thames at the wharves between Brook's and Three Cranes as marked on this 1875 plan.

barges were being turned round at Midhurst Wharf two or three times a week. Richard Isemonger's barges were advertised as leaving from Littlehampton 'by the canal' every Monday to Three Cranes Wharf, Upper Thames Street, while also loading two or three times a week at the Chichester Canal Basin.

The Guildford Almanack of 1836 gives the names of five barge-carriers, including that of Seward & Co., who were by now the leading carriers for most of Surrey and West Sussex. Most carriers owned only one or perhaps a pair of barges and generally served their particular neighbourhood. Nearly every riverside village boasted its own bargemaster. Names like Barnard of Petworth, Doick of Hardham, Henly of Bury, Nye of Pulborough, Seward of Loxwood, Smart of Offham, Stanton of Bramley, Stone of Pallingham, and Strudwick of Fittleworth were as familiar to the neighbourhood as those of

The wharves adjacent to Queenhithe, depicted here in 1851, were frequently advertised as points of dispatch for goods to Petworth and Midhurst. Seward & Co.'s barges left Chichester and Arundel two or three times a week bound for Queenhithe, while those of Richard Isemonger left Littlehampton every Monday for Three Cranes Wharf.

the baker, butcher and wheelwright. Most, if not all, were regular traders on the Rother Navigation.

From time to time requests were made to William Tyler for licences to build additional coal pens and sheds. Richard Isemonger of Littlehampton enquired if his lordship would permit him to build a house and make a coal yard at Midhurst: 'I send a great quantity of coals to Midhurst for sale and having barges continually loading with timber from that place for London, it would answer my purpose to have a coal yard.' Isemonger also took the opportunity of mentioning that 'he had a stack of well-seasoned timber and deals if you should be in want this year'.

In November 1837 Lord Egremont died. His three younger brothers had each predeceased him. Charles and William had both passed away in 1828, and Percy, the second eldest, who became Clerk of the Courts of Barbados, died unmarried in 1833 leaving William's son George heir to the earldom. Egremont appears to have had a good relationship with his nephew to whom in August 1831 he had transferred five of his shares in the Wey & Arun Junction Canal. Henry Edward Fox described Captain George Wyndham RN (1786–1845), who lived at Bramley in Surrey, as 'a coarse, vulgar, uneducated stupid man'.

On Lord Egremont's death the title and the Somerset estates went to the nephew, but most of his wealth was bequeathed to his three sons who took the name Wyndham by royal licence. All three had served with distinction in the Peninsular War and Henry commanded the detachment of Coldstream Guards which held Hougoumont at Waterloo.[88] However, it was the eldest son Colonel George Wyndham (1789–1869), who inherited Petworth, the Rother Navigation and his father's shareholdings in the Arun and the Wey & Arun waterways. All three concerns were approaching the zenith of their prosperity. Between 1837 and 1840 the Arun paid a dividend of 12 per cent and tolls averaged over £2,000 p.a. during the same period; likewise the Rother Navigation showed an operating profit of about £800 p.a.

Thomas Upton had been in charge of the navigation for forty-four years when Egremont died. He was also the Petworth Estate Manager responsible for looking after his lordship's house, stables, garden, parks, etc., as well as 'repairing farms, keeping in good order the woods, hatching the oak bark and paying bills'. For these responsibilities he received the substantial salary of £300 p.a. It is probable that he had handed over the day-to-day management to his younger brother Henry some years before, and as he was seventy-four at the time of Egremont's death,* Colonel Wyndham appointed Henry Upton in his place. When Henry Upton (sen.) died in 1840 aged sixty-eight, his son Henry (jun.) took over the management of the navigation.

The second John King, the toll collector at Fittleworth, died in October 1840 aged sixty-nine. His place was filled in 1841 on a permanent basis by Anthony Whitting, who had been born in the village in 1807. Whitting became a well-known local figure who supervised the wharf, the lock and collected the dues until at least 1862.† He and his family lived near the Swan Inn in a house which also served as the village grocery and remained so until the 1960s.

After the opening of the London to Brighton railway in 1841, preparations

---

* Thomas Poling Upton died on 7 September 1845, aged eighty-two.

† Kelly's Sussex trade directory of 1862. In later issues (until 1890) Whitting is simply recorded as a grocer and in the national census of 1891 as 'grocer retired'. His wife Mary died in 1875 aged seventy.

No. *223* · ROTHER NAVIGATION.

Name of Owner : *Stoveld* Number : *13*
Kind of Lading : *Coals*
Quantity : *50* Tons, Cwts.
Whence brought : *From the Arun*
Where to be landed : *Fittleworth*
Distance of Navigation : *5* Miles, *6* Furlongs.

	£	s	d
TONNAGE	2	3	1½
WHARFAGE	—	15	—
	2	10	1½

July 27/42 Toll-Collector.

Although timber and coal merchant William Stoveld died in 1841, the toll collector at Fittleworth continued to describe him as the barge-owner.

were begun to extend the railway to Chichester and Portsmouth. Although the project was favoured by the majority of traders and townspeople along the south coast, twenty petitions were entered against the bill, including those by the individual navigations and by George Wyndham. Wyndham, however, was loathe to pursue the matter through the House of Commons and replied to a plea by the commissioners of the Port of Arundel that he had 'no idea of taking measures alone to oppose this bill, although I object to it very much and have returned myself dissentient'.[89] It was therefore agreed that only the Arun Navigation proprietors and the Port of Arundel commissioners should retain counsel to support their petition against the bill before the House of Commons committee in 1844 (see *London's Lost Route to the Sea*, pp. 140–3).

There is some evidence that Colonel Wyndham took an interest in the Rother Navigation. In 1841, when he needed a supply of good hay, he looked into the possibility of barging it down from London. Mr Bonamy's

Received 3ᵈ *March* 18**43**

ROTHER

Navigation Tolls.

A. Whitting, Collector

per Henry Upton

From 27 Dec⁻ 42 **to** 17, Feby 18*43*

£	s	d
96	17	9

Every month or so Anthony Whitting, the lock-keeper and toll collector at Fittleworth, sent a list of all traffic and money received to Henry Upton at Petworth.

barge office at Arundel quoted 45s a ton for carriage to Coultershaw Wharf; it was explained that the best hay cost £5 11s and another 4s had to be allowed for bringing it up from the wharf to Petworth House. Attempts to ascertain how many tons of hay a barge could hold and the charge for carriage to Queenhithe or Three Cranes wharves produced no simple answer; in the end it was recommended to the London solicitors that it would be best to purchase hay from Colonel Wyndham's own corn and hay merchant at £5 8s a ton and to find a wharf like Hungerford Market or Scotland Yard 'where the hay could be put on the barge at once'.

Sometimes the goods delivered to Petworth House were not as good as they should be. In July 1842 Richard Isemonger had filled three barges at Littlehampton with coal from the packet *Cognac*. One of these, containing 24 tons of what was precisely termed 'Braddylls Hetton W.E. Coal', had been delivered by Goatcher ('Tyler's man') to Rotherbridge Wharf for Colonel Wyndham, but Upton reported to Tyler that they were 'very small and so much so that I cannot put them into the House but have ordered them to be laid out for your inspection until it can be settled what is to be done'.

Whereas Lord Egremont never presided over a general meeting of the Arun shareholders, Colonel Wyndham attended one at Arundel in December 1842. It was his only appearance. In 1844 he sent his agent Charles Murray as his proxy. Thereafter Henry Upton represented him from 1848 until his lordship's death in 1869. Upton attended at least one meeting and sometimes as many as four a year. Once, in 1852, when he was unable to attend, attorney Henry Brydone took his place. Althugh entries in Pigot's under Petworth and Midhurst only refer in general terms to the Rother Navigation, Seward & Co. are listed under Billingshurst as lime burners and coal merchants. In the 1839 edition this entry was altered to 'Seward, Child and Henly, coal and lime merchants and barge-owners. Newbridge Wharf'.

A freight ticket issued in 1840 reveals a further variation in title to the 'Chichester, Arundel, Petworth & Midhurst Barge Co.' In 1844, however, Child & Henly, an Arundel firm of coal merchants who already ran their own river barges, acquired Seward's fleet and consequently the London loading point was changed to Bull Wharf, near Upper Thames Street. Two years later, Thomas Bonamy & Son of Arundel took over the concern and in 1848 restored its former title, 'the Arundel Barge Co.'. Although the number of boats belonging to the company was now reduced to seven, Bonamys remained the principal carriers between London and Arundel until the 1860s.

It is interesting to note that the carriers disclaimed any liability for 'river piracy', which suggests that it was so widespread as to be almost regarded as inevitable. Certainly it was not uncommon for coal to be dropped overboard at certain places for the convenience of friends or relations, and if done in moderation it was usually impossible to detect the theft. More pernicious was the substitution of stone for coal to escape detection of the shortfall by the index.

The period from 1823 to 1863 marked the heyday of the Rother Navigation, when the annual tonnage never fell below 10,000. However, the tranquillity of the river was rarely disturbed. It was rare for more than five barges to pass in or out of the navigation on any one day and the average was about two. Even so, the wharves at Coultershaw and Midhurst were normally stacked high with timber awaiting shipment and heaped with coal ready for disposal.

Improved dredging and maintenance allowed barges to carry greater loads. In 1843 single cargoes of 45 tons were being delivered to Rotherbridge and 43 to Midhurst. However, an analysis of traffic in 1843 (see Appendix 4) shows that the average load up was 24 tons and only 21 tons down.* At this time the navigation was used by twenty-six bargemasters controlling fifty-seven barges which made a total of 535 voyages up and down the river. Henly of Bury operated seven barges and the Smart family at Houghton another six.

---

* In 1814 the heaviest cargo had been 37 tons, but the average was 25 tons up and 21¼ tons down.

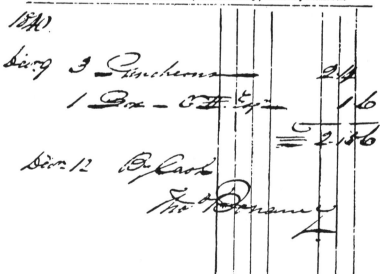

Invoice issued by the Chichester, Arundel, Petworth & Midhurst Barge Company
in 1840 and signed by Thomas Bonamy.

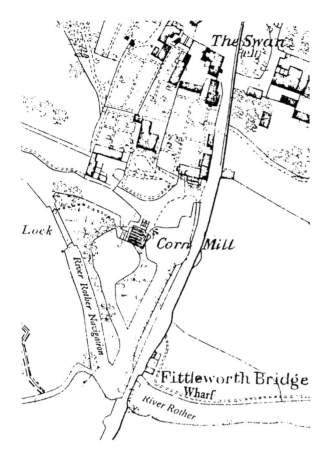

Fittleworth Wharf and Lock,
1876.

On the Rother itself there was now only the odd carrier. William Stoveld's fleet had been dispersed after his decease two years before. His executors had retained one barge, Richard Goatcher of Petworth had acquired two, and Edmund Wackford a fourth. The remainder had gone further afield.

As the population grew along the Rother Valley so did the needs of the inhabitants. The size of Petworth increased by half between 1801 and 1851 and even villages like Fittleworth and Selham grew by at least a third. In 1843 the quantity of coal being discharged had risen to 2,000 tons and all in all 7,000 tons of merchandise passed through Coultershaw that year, which represented 55 per cent of the total traffic.

Midhurst remained the second most important port with the movement of 3,000 tons, while the tonnage moved at other wharves was as follows:

Lodsbridge	940 tons
Fittleworth	540 tons
Rotherbridge	510 tons
Shopham	496 tons
Coates	65 tons
Poyntzs'	38 tons
Ambersham	36 tons

At Lodsbridge a part-time wharfinger was employed while the toll collector continued to act as both lock-keeper and wharfinger at Fittleworth.

Upstream traffic was three times heavier than down; consequently two out of every three barges proceeding towards Midhurst descended empty. Coal and chalk were the predominant up cargoes, timber, bark and hoops the principal down. Bricks from Harwoods Green, seaweed from Littlehampton and a variety of different types of groceries were brought from London either by way of Guildford and the Wey & Arun Junction Canal, or via Arundel and the coastal route.

There was very little interchange of goods between the wharves on the Rother itself. At least very little was paid in tolls, which could only be collected at Fittleworth, so that a barge could technically pass between Coultershaw and Ambersham or Midhurst without being asked to pay. However, it is unlikely that this occurred very often, although the fact remains that in 1843, for instance, tolls were paid on only 30½ tons of local traffic to

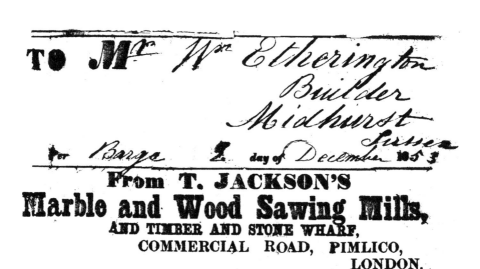

Barge delivery note to Midhurst, 1853.

Midhurst – 23 tons of manure from Fittleworth, 1½ tons of timber from Coultershaw and 6 tons from Shopham.

Ninety per cent of the Rother's traffic originated from below Pulborough and less than 10 per cent from above Newbridge. However, 25 per cent of the Rother's downward traffic passed through the junction canal to the Wey Navigation. Cargoes averaged 15 tons and sometimes exceeded 30 and 35 tons. The problem was to obtain return goods in sufficient quantity to make such traffic profitable. Consignments of groceries averaged only 7 tons or so and there was little other merchandise to be found.

As the table below shows the pattern of traffic in the 1840s did not differ greatly from that of the 1820s:

Principal Cargoes　　　　　　　　　*Annual Tonnage*

	1822	1832	1843	Average for ten years*
Coal (incl. culm)	3,814	5,012	5,301	4,650
Timber (incl. bark)	1,583	1,677	1,831	2,357†
Chalk	1,111	1,976	2,280	1,670
Seaweed	1,552	318	464	831
Groceries	417	318	408	426
Hoops (incl. spokes)	88	378	340	359
Stone	111	23	170	310
Corn & Flour	97	376	319	290
Lime	159	598	386	290
Ashes	184	180	nil	260
Sand	110	85	371	160
Bricks & Tiles	37	190	300	140
Bog Earth	32	103	nil	75
Slate	20	52	98	44
TOTAL	9,750	11,800	12,627	

The attitude of the barge-owners to the opening of the railway from London to Guildford in 1844 may be likened to that of sea-ferry operators faced with the opening of the Channel Tunnel. In January 1845 the barge-

---

* For the ten years between 1822 and 1843 where details are available.

† The timber traffic rose to 3,831 and 4,291 tons in 1824 and 1825 respectively.

owners and sundry timber merchants, millers and coal merchants met in the council chamber at Guildford whereupon it was unanimously agreed to petition the Wey Navigation proprietors for toll reductions on the grounds that they were much too high in view of the increased facilities of turnpike roads and railroads. It was argued that a reduced toll on timber 'would cause the timber which now goes to Arundel from the neighbourhood of Pulborough, Petworth and Midhurst' be brought by inland navigation to London. Indeed, it was pointed out that the canal company had agreed to make a special reduction on a 'certain large quantity of timber coming from the Midhurst River'.[90] It was thought that linseed oil, cake for cattle feed, groceries, iron, rags for manure and paper-making were other items, currently carried up by land, which could be attracted to water transport.

Fears were also expressed that the forthcoming completion of the Brighton & Chichester railway would cripple the through trade to Arundel. It was these fears that prompted the Wey and Wey & Arun navigations to substantially reduce their tolls in an effort to retain the heavy traffic of coal, chalk and timber. Subsequently some of this traffic was wrested back from the railway during the 1850s.

After 1863 barges continued to pass between the Rother Navigation and the Thames on a desultory basis until the closure of the connecting link in 1871. The traffic ledgers are no longer available, but evidence by opponents of the Abandonment Bill before the House of Lords committee in 1868 stressed the continued importance of water transport for moving timber from the Rother Valley to Godalming and the Thames (see Chapter Eleven).

One of the last Rother barges to pass through the Wey & Arun Junction Canal was the *Eleanor*. She belonged to John Strudwick (1820–1903) of Fittleworth, who had worked as a youth on the Portsmouth & Arundel Canal.[91] Her usual trips were to Littlehampton laden with brick clay, returning with coal for Fittleworth and Petworth.

On occasions, bargemaster Daniel Wakeford (1843–1913) would be sent on more adventurous voyages to places beyond London. Loaded with powderwood (alder) at Midhurst, the *Eleanor* would proceed to Weybridge and Teddington before dropping down with the tide to Limehouse Cut, while the horse walked through London to meet her. The journey was then resumed up the River Lea to the munitions factory at Waltham Abbey in Essex. The trip lasted ten days, which sounds incredible in its leisured slowness, but as Lady Maxse pointed out, even in the 1930s trucks of wood billets dispatched by goods train from Midhurst to Waltham Abbey generally took ten days to arrive. In April 1871 *Eleanor* made her last trip through the Wey & Arun after collecting 19 tons of timber stacked at Dapdune Wharf, Guildford.

CHAPTER TEN

THE COMING OF THE RAILWAYS (1857–66)

Mid-Sussex Railway Act (1857) – the Rother Navigation profits from the carriage of building materials – opening of railway to Pulborough and Petworth (1859) – opening of Midhurst gasworks (1861) – opening of railway from Pulborough to Ford (1863) – from Guildford to Horsham (1865) – from Petworth to Midhurst (1866).

The first railway in Sussex was opened in 1840. It is often assumed that the canal companies opposed every rival railway bill. Some did, but very few succeeded; however, the early acts often gave so much protection or consideration to landowners and rival concerns that the railway companies were bound sooner or later to press for less onerous conditions. For example, in 1844 the Arun Navigation was able to protect its right of passage against the Shoreham to Chichester line by requiring the railway company to provide a drawbridge over the river at Ford with a 63 ft opening section. This had to be kept open one and a half hours before and after high water except for ten minutes before and four minutes after train times. The railway company was also liable to pay a £10 fine if any barge was detained longer than twenty minutes. Not until an amending Act was passed in 1860 were these requirements modified and not until 1938 was a fixed bridge built.

As soon as the need for a railway became evident, however, all a canal company could do was to negotiate the best terms possible. The Wey & Arun Canal management committee tried to reach an accommodation with the London, Brighton & South Coast Railway. The railway company's minutes reveal that early in 1859 a plan was conceived to convert 16 miles of the canal into a railway. On 4 August a deputation, led by John Napper the chairman of the Wey & Arun, met the directors of the LB & SCR to seek their views on the proposal to build a railway to link Guildford with Pulborough along the line of the existing canal. However, when it was discovered that no survey had been carried out, the LB & SCR informed the promoters that they would not form a definite opinion unless a 'matured scheme' was submitted that appeared practicable and had the support of owners of agricultural land who would grant 'every facility to sell the land at agricultural prices'. There is no further mention of the canal conversion scheme and the Wey & Arun Canal Company's draft minute book makes no reference to this proposal, although on 14 February 1860 the seven members of the committee

In spite of determined opposition from the Arun Navigation Proprietors, the London & Brighton Railway Company obtained its Act in 1844 to build a line from Shoreham to Chichester, which involved building this drawbridge across the Arun at Ford. The telescopic bridge had a 60 ft opening which took two men and a boy at least five minutes to open. The single track timber bridge was replaced by a double track sliding bridge in 1862.

of management with Napper in the chair resolved that no opposition be offered to the bill for the Horsham to Guildford railway which obtained its Act that year.

As the 1860s drew near, the expansion of the network of railways in Surrey continued apace and plans were afoot to construct three branch lines which would come into direct competition with the Arun and Rother navigations. The first to be built was the Mid-Sussex line from Horsham to Pulborough and Petworth, whose Act was passed in 1857. The Arun proprietors had tried to come to some arrangement with the railway company and rather optimistically had offered to withdraw their opposition to the bill if the company would agree to make up any deficiency between receipts and expenditure of the navigation, which prevented the payment of a 5 per cent dividend in any year after the opening of the railway. Since only 5½ per cent had been paid for the previous year it was hardly surprising that this offer was not even entertained; the only alternative was for the Arun to petition against the bill in an attempt to procure compensation. In this they were entirely unsuccessful, the House of Lords committee ruling that the canal company had no right to be heard against the preamble, only the clauses.

The promoters had originally intended to build their line from Horsham to Billingshurst with branches to Petworth and Pulborough. However, this former branch, which would have crossed 18 ft above the Arun Canal, a short distance above Orfold Lock, was strongly opposed by Colonel Wyndham on the grounds of the intended line's proximity to Petworth House. Consequently, the line was made direct to Pulborough and built along the south bank of the Rother via Hardham to Petworth. The River Arun was bridged by a single span of 120 ft at Pulborough, and Hardham Canal Tunnel crossed only 8 ft above its crown. As a result the Rother Navigation and the Petworth Estate were spared interference, but the townspeople of Petworth had a long walk to the station, which was situated south of Coultershaw Wharf and 2 miles from the town.

The building of the railway along the Rother Valley increased traffic on the navigation as barge after barge brought ballast, bricks and sleepers to landing places within 100 or so yards of its would-be competitor. As a consequence tolls rose from £894 in 1855 to £1,231 in 1857 and totalled £1,274 during 1858, the highest amount to be recorded in its history.

The railway was opened from Pulborough to Fittleworth and Petworth in October 1859. The immediate effect on the navigation's commerce was insignificant. Indeed, the building of the Mid-Sussex branch also brought increased revenue to both the Arun Navigation and the Wey & Arun Canal, and even when completed it took little traffic from the Rother or from the Arun for whom the main blow was the authorization, on 23 July 1860, of the extension from Hardham through the Arun Valley to Ford by the LB & SCR (Deviations) Act. However, this new line brought one benefit to the Arun Navigation. In order to save the expense of two swing bridges over the sharp bend in the river at Offham, the railway company decided to cut a new channel for the river, which, while enabling it to build fixed bridges, reduced the distance by water between Bury Wharf and Arundel by nearly a mile.

An unexpected boost to the Rother Navigation's trade resulted from the decision to build the gasworks at Midhurst on land adjacent to the wharf. The formation of the Midhurst Gas Company with a paid up capital of £4,000 caused the carriage of building materials during 1860 to be followed after its opening in 1861 by the need for a regular supply of coal. Because the railway was only open to Petworth, barges from Arundel came up once or twice a week to Midhurst.

The navigation was fortunate that, unlike many other waterways, its location and the nature of its main traffic caused it to suffer little competition from improved land carriage. Indeed, tolls on the Rother continued to exceed £1,000 p.a. until 1862 in which year the navigation carried a record 16,500 tons.

It was the opening of the Mid-Sussex line from Pulborough to Amberley, Arundel and Ford on 3 August 1863, followed a fortnight later by the branch to Littlehampton, which caused the Rother Navigation to lose 5,000 tons or 40 per cent of its annual traffic. As a result the receipts of both the Arun and the Rother navigations fell dramatically. In 1864 tolls on the Rother fell by over a third while the Arun Navigation was forced to cut its dividend by a third in 1865.

RIVER ARUN NAVIGATION,

(Twelve Miles)

Tolls to be Charged from the 1st of August, 1856.

UP TOLLS.

		£	s.	d.
PER TON	Coal, Culm, and Slate, from Arundel to the Wey ...	0	0	9
	Coal to Elmbridge Wharf	0	0	9
	Ditto to Drungwick and Loxwood	0	1	8
	Ditto to Newbridge	0	1	8
	Culm to ditto	0	1	3
	Seed Cake and Corn to ditto	0	2	0
PER KILN	Lime to ditto	0	6	0
PER TON	Large Chalk to ditto	0	0	6
	Kiln ditto to ditto	0	0	4
	Chalk Grit, Flints, Gravel, and Sand to ditto	0	0	6
	Flint, and Stone for building, to ditto	0	1	0
	Lime and Soap Ashes	0	1	0
	Timber from Arundel to ditto	0	2	0
	Hoops, Bark, and Timber from Hardham, Stopham, and Pallingham to the Wey	0	1	0
	Hoops and Bark, Wharfage from Newbridge to the Wey	0	1	0
PER LOAD	Timber from Newbridge to the Wey, Wharfage and Drawing	0	2	6
PER HUN.	Spokes, Wharfage	0	0	6
PER TON	Merchandize Goods from Arundel and the Rother into the Wey and Arun	0	1	0

PER LOAD	Timber converted, &c., at Newbridge Wharf	0	1	0
PER TON	Storing and delivering Cake, Manure, &c., at Newbridge Store	0	1	0
	Bark stored at Newbridge Wharf for every entire 3 months and for any less period than 3 months	0	1	0
	For shooting and Storing Bark	0	1	0
	For Stored Bark, to pay on Delivery	0	1	0

Railway and road competition forced the canal companies to reduce their tolls in the 1840s and '50s. By 1856 the Arun Canal and the Rother Navigation charged only one third of the amount levied on coal in the 1820s.

RIVER ARUN NAVIGATION,

(Twelve Miles)

Tolls to be Charged from the 1st of August, 1856.

DOWN TOLLS.

	£	s.	d.
PER TON Merchandize Goods from the Wey and Arun to the Rother or Arundel	0	1	0
Timber, Plank, &c. from the Wey to Arundel ...	0	1	0
Ditto from Elmbridge, Compasses, Tickner's Heath, and Jinnets	0	1	0
Ditto from Drungwick and Loxwood	0	1	6
Ditto from Newbridge Wharf, including Wharfage and Drawing	0	2	6
Posts and Rails from Newbridge	0	2	0
Malt and Corn from ditto	0	2	0
Bark or Hoops from ditto	0	2	0
Ditto from Loxwood	0	2	0
For all Goods brought from the Wey and Arun, and Landed at Newbridge Wharf	0	1	0
Hoops from the Rother, or elsewhere, stacked at Newbridge Wharf	0	1	0

TUNNEL TOLLS.

	£	s.	d.
PER TON Passing to and fro, including Coldwaltham Brook ...			
Timber, Bark, Hoops, Coal, Culm, Corn, Lime, and Merchandize Goods	0	0	6
Large Chalk	0	0	4
Kiln Chalk, Grit, Ashes, &c.	0	0	3
Stone for Building	0	0	6
Stone, Flint, Gravel for Roads, Sand, and all Kinds of Manure	0	0	3
Corn to Hardham Mill	0	0	3

JAMES POWELL,

Clerk.

The list of toll charges indicates that all coal came up from Littlehampton and none down from London. The timber traffic was substantial in both directions.

Fittleworth Wharf from the painting by Henry Moore, 1865.

Observe the simple gang plank, the pole and the bowler hats worn by the bargemen.

The railway linked London to Midhurst in only two hours compared with three days by water.

The extension of the railway to Midhurst in 1866 resulted in further toll reductions in an effort to retain the coal traffic; consequently tolls dropped to below £500 for the year, the lowest since 1799. Even so, while traffic from the Wey to the Rother was stated by a witness before a House of Lords committee in 1868 to be 'very little indeed', from the Rother northwards it remained 'very considerable'.[92] This was perhaps a slight exaggeration, but it was a fact that the railway company refused to carry very large logs or tree trunks which they said were too dangerous or inconvenient. Consequently these continued to be moved either by road or by water, and it was the threatened loss of the timber trade which was the main reason why both the Arun and the Godalming navigations opposed the bill to abandon the Wey & Arun Junction Canal, when the bill was introduced into the House of Lords in February 1868.

CHAPTER ELEVEN

DECLINE AND FALL (1866–88)

Joint management of the Rother and Arun navigations – traffic in the 1860s – the Wey & Arun Junction Canal Abandonment Bill (1868) – attempts by the Arun Navigation to retain the link to the Thames – Lord Leconfield's impartiality – evidence before the House of Lords committee – closure of the Wey & Arun Junction Canal (1871) – effect on the Arun and Rother navigations traffic – efforts made to keep open the Arun Navigation – Lord Leconfield agrees to help – subscribes to the Arun Navigation Appeal (1883) – last toll reductions (1885) – closure of the Arun Canal and Rother Navigation (1888).

At some time in the 1850s or '60s the Rother and Arun navigations may have come under one management; Dashwood stated in 1867 that this was the case.[93] If so it seems possible that Colonel Wyndham (created Lord Leconfield in 1859) decided to leave the day-to-day business to the Arun Navigation's superintendent. This may have occurred when, or soon after, John Sprinks took up the post in 1857. In 1868 Richard Holmes referred to him as having 'a great number of offices combined in one', but did not list them.[94] It is unlikely, however, that he had much to do with the Rother Navigation as there is no mention of his name in the extant Rother papers. The Arun minute books are silent on the subject and between 1863 and 1884 there is no debit entry for management expenses in the Rother accounts. Between 1870 and 1874 all expenditure on repairs is in the name of a Mr R. Downing. It may therefore have been rather a loose arrangement. In 1869 the dying peer arranged for both Upton and Henry Brydone to purchase one £100 share in the Arun Navigation for £50. When the next transfer of shares was recorded in 1872, the bargain was struck at £7.

The existing records of the navigation after 1848 are fragmentary. However, any reduction in traffic resulting from the general economic situation and the development of local railways in the late 1850s had little impact on the daily traffic on the navigation, whose annual carriage averaged 14,000 tons from 1840 to 1863. What did occur was a population shift from the area. Between the 1851 and 1861 census, the population of Arundel, Easebourne, Hardham, Littlehampton, Lodsworth, Midhurst, Petworth, South Ambersham and Stopham all declined.

As mentioned in Chapter Ten, it was not until the opening of railway communication through the Arun Valley from Pulborough to Littlehampton that traffic on the waterway greatly deteriorated. The Wey & Arun Junction Canal Company's profitability was also seriously impaired by the opening of the Horsham to Guildford railway in October 1865. In 1866, however, when the management committee proposed to abandon the canal, both the Arun Navigation shareholders and the commissioners of the Godalming Navigation were seriously concerned at the loss of their connecting link. While talks were held to decide the future of the Wey & Arun Junction Canal, Lord Leconfield remained ambivalent: on the one hand he was the largest shareholder in a canal company which was in serious decline and which a small majority of the other shareholders wished to wind up; on the other he was a major shareholder in the Arun Navigation besides being the proprietor of the Rother Navigation, both of which would lose a substantial amount of traffic if the canal was closed. In the two years 1866 and 1867, over one third of the Arun Navigation's tolls came from the canal: 3,444 tons in 1866 and 4,794 in 1867.

Henry Brydone, Lord Leconfield's agent, attended committee of management meetings on his behalf but did not vote or use his proxy. William Smallpeice, the clerk to the Wey & Arun Canal, was asked in the House of Lords whether Lord Leconfield had assented to the course adopted by the majority of the proprietors to close the canal and replied: 'We never took any step without consulting him. He consented to everything that was done.'[95] This was probably the case; his lordship had advised the clerk that if the majority of the shareholders wished to wind up the company, he would fall in with their wishes.

In November 1866 Richard Holmes had had a long discussion with Henry Brydone when they travelled together from Petworth to attend a canal company meeting at Guildford, which concluded, according to Holmes, with him assuring Brydone that the Arun proprietors were willing to vote part of their funds to keep the Wey & Arun open. Furthermore, he claimed that it was Brydone who had stated at one meeting how very desirable it was to keep the canal open. When the Wey & Arun committee met again in January 1867, Holmes's resolution that the Arun Navigation should contribute an annual sum to enable the canal to remain open was voted down and it was this action which prompted the petitions by the Arun Navigation and others to oppose the Wey & Arun Junction Canal (Abandonment) Bill. Lord Leconfield took no action.

The hearing before a select committee of the House of Lords in March 1868 lasted three days during which ten witnesses were called. These included John Sprinks, manager of the Arun Navigation, Thomas Pullen, the former superintendent of the Wey & Arun, and Thomas Isemonger, the bargemaster from Littlehampton who stated that he had 1,000 tons of timber waiting to be barged from Arundel to Godalming.

Seven petitions were entered against the bill. The London, Brighton & South Coast Railway sought powers to transform the viaduct at Whipley Manor into an embankment. The commissioners of the Port of Arundel, the Wey (Godalming) commissioners and the proprietors of the Arun Navigation opposed the bill on the grounds that traffic from the Thames and the Wey would be lost to their navigations. The landowners adjoining the canal were concerned at the prospect of their fields being flooded should the embankments collapse and by the loss of the tow-path which served as a passage for cattle between enclosures. Lord Grantley was perturbed at the cost of filling in his section of the canal at Wonersh Park.

What prejudiced the case of the promoters of the bill was their failure to come to some understanding with the parties opposing the bill. One witness, a solicitor on the Wey & Arun management committee, cross-examined by counsel for the commissioners of the Port of Arundel, was forced to admit that he did not know what annual sum would be required to keep the canal open; only that £120 p.a. would not be enough. This response prompted one of the Law Lords to interrupt: 'Cannot you say what would pay you?', to which the solicitor lamely replied: 'I have no doubt that we should very soon get at it.' But, responded counsel, do you really expect their lordships to 'pass this tub to a whale without defining what the sum is?'[96] The point was doubly made.

After the tenth witness had been called, the chairman Lord Methuen intimated that they had heard enough. On the third day the bill's opponents secured the insertion of seven additional clauses whose effect was to allow a reprieve for the Wey & Arun if certain conditions were fulfilled. The petitioners for the bill agreed as a compromise that the canal should not be closed or sold in lots before 30 September 1869 if, within six months from the granting of the Act, sufficient money was guaranteed for running expenses; furthermore, that if the canal were disposed of in its entirety, it should not be sold back to the riparan owners until it had been closed for traffic for six consecutive months.

During the proceedings in the House of Lords reference was made to the traffic passing from the Rother Navigation through the Wey & Arun Canal. Richard Holmes, the clerk to the commissioners of the Port of Arundel who were shareholders in the canal company, stated that 'a good deal of timber is now cut upon the Cowdray Estate which is now being conveyed at the present time up through the Wey & Arun'. Another witness stated that the timber traffic passed along the Wey & Arun in both directions and that 'the size governs which way it goes. Soft woods imported from Scandinavia came down from the Thames while oak, elm and beech went up.'[97]

In 1869 the first Lord Leconfield died leaving his shares in the Wey & Arun and the Arun to his eldest son Henry Wyndham. Although the Abandonment Act had been passed, it was not inevitable that the Wey & Arun Canal should be closed if a purchaser could be found. Meanwhile a small and fairly regular traffic continued to use the waterway. Tolls actually increased slightly during the year ending April 1868, when the navigation's abandonment was being so actively discussed. This may have been due to the Guildford to Horsham railway raising its charges for the carriage of goods soon after its opening, and for a while it seemed that the canal might retain sufficient traffic to warrant its continued upkeep. However, no resuscitation occurred and tolls dwindled to £393 and £359 in 1869 and 1870 respectively. In August 1870 the Wey & Arun Junction Canal was put up for auction at Guildford as a going concern. There were no bidders and a last-ditch offer by the Arun Navigation in December to take a repairing lease was rejected. In May 1871 Vice-Chancellor Sir Richard Malins ordered notice of the proposal to close the canal to be advertised. After a hearing in chambers, the judge ordered the link between London and Midhurst to be formally broken with effect from 22 July 1871.

Little consideration was given during the passage of canal bills, or indeed of the later railway bills, as to what should happen when the line ceased to be used. The only value of a derelict canal was the land together with the buildings, which had to be offset against any public liability for the maintenance of bridges carrying public highways and so forth. Whatever the position there was usually little or no money left to pay for maintenance, and once any buildings had been sold the riparian landowners often refused to buy back and accept the responsibility of owning a ready channel which could prove more of a liability than an asset. As the former canal company had no obligation or finance available to fill in the old channel, the abandoned canal was left to nature. Attempts were made by the official liquidator to sell the land, but even when the company was formally dissolved in 1910, there were still stretches of the canal bed which no one was willing to purchase.

The effect of the canal closure was exactly what the Arun proprietors had feared. Although toll receipts had held up around £450 p.a. between 1869 and 1872, in 1873 they fell by nearly half. The Rother was more seriously affected as receipts dipped by 30 per cent in 1872 and by a further 15 per cent in each of the next two successive years.

Both navigations introduced economies. The Arun Navigation Company ceased to act as wharfingers at Newbridge in 1874. Wages were reduced, staff

A barge moored below Fittleworth Bridge, 1875, from a watercolour by A.W. Weedon.

This photograph was taken at Newbridge about 1885, after the Wey & Arun Canal had been closed. Frederick and Walter were the sons of the wharfinger, George Dunkerton.

ARUN NAVIGATION.

NOTICE.

The Navigation will be

CLOSED

on and from the 1st day of January, 1888, the Traffic being insufficient to meet the working expenses.

BY ORDER,

Chichester,

13th December, 1887.

EDWARD ARNOLD,

CLERK.

ADCOCK. PRINTER, NORTH STREET, CHICHESTER.

Barge traffic on the Arun Canal gradually declined after the closing of the Wey & Arun Canal in 1871. Although the navigation remained open until 1888, the company announced it would cease to be wharfingers in 1874.

made redundant. The state of the works gradually deteriorated, and when the proprietors made their annual inspection by barge in 1882 it was observed that parts of the canal were falling into decay. Although the second Lord Leconfield was still the second largest shareholder he took no active part in its day-to-day affairs. However, in September, with regard to the navigation's future, his agent wrote: 'we all of us think that his Lordship is really much more interested in the question than anyone else'. Consequently a meeting was held at Petworth House to discuss the future of both navigations. The consensus opinion was that while there was little likelihood of any material revival of business, keeping the navigations open kept down the railway rates and was therefore in the public interest. Lord Leconfield took the chair at a meeting in Pulborough in February 1884 at which the proprietors and landowners were invited to subscribe £50 or so a year toward the cost of keeping the Arun Navigation open. Lord Leconfield subscribed £10, Sir Walter Barttelot of Stopham House and Richard Holmes of Arundel each £5, but only nominal sums were received from four or five others.

In December 1884 a final effort was made to revive trade when both the Arun and Rother reduced the toll on coal to 3*d* a ton for 1885 to enable the bargemen to compete with the railway. The experiment lasted two years, but the extent to which traffic could be taken from the railway was limited although it is believed that the Midhurst gasworks were the main beneficiaries of this concession.

In 1884 – the last year when traffic figures are available – the Rother Navigation carried about 1,600 tons compared with the Arun Navigation's 4,500. In 1887, the Arun Navigation's uncelebrated centenary year, the figure had fallen to little more than 2,000 tons. A final appeal by the chairman to shareholders met with little response. As expenses now exceeded receipts, notices were posted announcing the closure of the canal from 1 January 1888. However, in spite of this announcement the navigation remained open to any traffic which presented itself. On 20 June 1888 the last load of chalk left Houghton, 10 tons for Lee Farm and 20 for Newbridge. In the autumn some empty barges were taken up to Newbridge to be broken up. Some months later in January 1889 the last barge passed through Hardham Tunnel.

CHAPTER TWELVE

UNOFFICIALLY ABANDONED (1888–1936)

Pleasure boating – Port's boathouse at Midhurst – Prothero & Clarke's Cruising Manual (1896) – Warrant of Abandonment issued for the Arun Navigation (1896) – Hardham Tunnel blocked (1898) – Egmont v. Leconfield dispute (1903) – Bonthron's trip down the Rother (c. 1905) – Eleanor Barnes – her winter canoe voyage – application to Ministry of Transport to close the navigation (1935) – Warrant of Abandonment issued (1936).

Although barge traffic had ceased on the Rother in March 1888, stretches of the navigation were still used occasionally by pleasure boats as they had been in the days of the 3rd earl.[98] The first references to boating on the Rother date from July 1818, when Mr Philpot made three excursions in his pleasure boat passing through Todham Lock as far as Moorland Lock. There are also details of tolls paid in 1822 and 1825 and mention of Lord Egremont's boathouse, which stood below Rotherbridge by Spershotts Hanger, being repaired. It was not until 1857, when the second edition of the *Oarman's Guide to the Thames* informed the aquatic public that a trip from the Isis to the Rother was a feasible proposition, that pleasure boats ventured up the river. Even so, there are no accounts of boating expeditions until after the navigation was closed.

The passion for boating by the Victorians was a phenomenon which developed during the closing decades of the nineteenth century. In the days before the advent of the motor car, boating was a pleasant alternative to taking out the pony and trap, watching cricket or playing croquet or lawn tennis. The pastime had been claiming an increasing number of devotees as a 'day on the river' began to extend to excursions lasting several weeks or more.[99]

The Thames was the scene of most boating expeditions as exemplified by Jerome K. Jerome's *Three Men in a Boat* (1889), but its tributaries were also a lure to the adventurous. In 1867 J.B. Dashwood had pioneered the first recorded family holiday afloat on British canals, when he had voyaged with his wife and dog through the Wey & Arun Junction Canal *en route* to watch the naval review, held at Spithead in honour of the Sultan of Turkey's state visit. It had been quite an eventful trip. There had been lock-gates difficult to open, bullocks threatening the party at Shalford, and shortly after observing

Midhurst canal basin in about 1912, after Mr Port's boathouse had burnt down.

the entrance to the Rother Navigation a nasty accident had been narrowly averted in Hardham Lock.[100]

The popularity of boating grew year by year. Tolls from pleasure boats on the Wey Navigation in Surrey amounted to £30 in 1870, but had increased tenfold by 1890 and, after an exceptionally fine summer, totalled £371 in 1893, a figure which increased receipts from commercial traffic by one third. In 1895 the *New Guide Book to Midhurst & the Neighbourhood* mentioned that the navigation had been superceded by the railway for the carriage of merchandise, but drew attention to the fact that the beautiful scenery offered an excellent opportunity for aquatic excursions and fishing. Boats, it stated, could be obtained at the wharf of Mr Port.

William Port (1871–1923) was actually a plumber by trade and it was his mother who owned the boats. It was she who encouraged her son to improve the family's finances by letting out skiffs. This small boating station continued in use for many years and provided a source of enjoyment to many local people both young and old. Doubtless, it would have continued to do so had not a fire destroyed the boathouse in 1912. Craft, however, rarely ventured downstream beyond the shallows at Todham Lock and only once did Port apparently let a boat for a through journey (see page 147).

Row boats could also be hired at Coultershaw Wharf and Fittleworth as well as at Stopham and Pulborough on the Arun. Several riparian landowners kept a skiff or punt for their families and friends but, as Lady Maxse observed, the social amenities of Fittleworth suffered greatly from the abandonment. The locks fell into disrepair and boating became almost impossible. The Hon. Mary Maxse (1870–1944), sister of Lord Leconfield, remembered how in her childhood she had spent long summer days punting between the banks laden with meadowsweet and codlings-and-cream, and setting or taking up nightlines in the tumbling bays which lay alongside the locks. She also reflected that 'at least one boat was swept over the mill sluice gates at floodtime, while its occupants barely escaped with their lives'.[101]

The first comprehensive guidebook to the waterways of the British Isles was published in 1896 when Prothero & Clarke's *A New Oarsman's Guide* appeared. The description of each navigation, with details of distances, locks, towns and accommodation, revealed interesting facts about the state of every waterway although, as the editors pointed out, time was continually working changes. 'Navigations fell to pieces, channels altered or were silted up, mills and weirs disappeared, old inns were closed or changed their character along with their owners.'

Sadly, by 1896 most of the Sussex navigations had fallen into disuse. However, the guide emphasized that the whole course of the Rother was through 'an exceedingly beautiful valley between wooded slopes and beech-clad hills'. Canoes, it was claimed, could descend from Iping, 19 miles above Stopham, when the river was full. Entries gave snippets of local information: that the landlord of the Angel Hotel could cart one's boat from Midhurst station; that Mr Port kept a few skiffs for hire at the wharf; and that now (1894) none of the locks was workable so that seven portages were necessary between Midhurst and Stopham. Advice was given that the entrance to Moorland Lock was 'sometimes choked with weeds and difficult to see', but that one should on no account go round by the backwater as it was 'blocked by fallen trees and a low bridge'; at Lodsbridge clay reefs threatened to capsize the unwary below the lock. Kelsham Floating Bridge, which was chained to the left bank, could be easily moved. George Lamboll, the Petworth carrier, would take a canoe from Coultershaw to Guildford any Friday for 5s. Shopham Lock, however, could be easily shot. 'Before doing so land and reconnoitre as on a full river snags sometimes get jammed athwart the entrance.' The miller at Fittleworth would house one's boat while a visit was made to the Swan Inn '(good 1894)'. Mention was made that it was a great

Miles		
	Iping Bridge	
2	Stedham Mill -	Portage.
4	Woolbeding Mill -	Portage.
$6\frac{3}{4}$	Midhurst Mill -	Portage. For next mile and a half the route is through Cowdray Park.
$7\frac{1}{4}$	Midhurst Wharf -	Under little bridge, right bank. Stats. L. & S. W. and L. B. & S. C. Rs. Hotel, Angel. Landlord can cart boat from station. Cowdray Park (Earl of Egmont) always open and Cowdray Ruins worth seeing.
9	Todham Lock -	Portage right bank. The lower gates having been removed the upper are converted into sluice gates.
$10\frac{1}{4}$	Moorland Lock -	Lock-cut sharp to left just above the sluice. Entrance is sometimes choked with weeds and difficult to see. On no account go round by backwater, which is blocked by fallen trees and low bridge.
11	Lodge Bridge Lock	Lock-cut is narrow channel by left bank. The broader one on right leads to Selham, a pretty village (Stat. L. B. & S. C. R.) Look out for clay-reefs in channel below.
$12\frac{1}{4}$	Lady Weir - -	Lower boat down wall side at right of sluice. Picturesque spot.
$13\frac{1}{2}$	Kelsham Floating Bridge - -	Chained to left bank. Easily moved (1894). Pretty reaches below.
$14\frac{7}{8}$	Coultershaw Lock -	Stat. L. B. & S. C. R. (right bank). Lock-cut on the right blocked (1894). Go on straight to mill, take out on right bank, carry along road to the right and launch from meadow. Petworth village $1\frac{1}{2}$ mile left bank. Petworth House (Earl of Egremont) has fine paintings, sculpture, &c.; open on Thursdays. George Lamboll, carrier, Petworth, goes to Guildford every Friday, and will take canoe from Coultershaw Bridge to the Wey (p. 11) or *vice versa* for 5s.
$15\frac{7}{8}$	Shopham Lock -	Strong stream in lock-cut. Lock has no gates and water rushes through. Can be easily shot. Before doing so land and reconnoitre, as on a full river snags sometimes get jammed athwart entrance. From here to Fittleworth more open but still beautiful country.
Miles 18	Fittleworth Lock -	Stat. L. B. & S. C. R. Lock-cut blocked. Go on to mill and portage on left bank. Look out for stones below mill. Inn, Swan (good 1894). Great place for artists. See room with painted panels and "Visitors' Book." Miller can house boat.
$19\frac{1}{2}$	Stopham Lock -	Lock-cut was (1894) blocked by felled trees —probably only temporarily. It is possible to go over little weir on right at entrance to cut and by backwater ($1\frac{1}{4}$ mile) to Hardham Mill Lock, where is easy portage close to Arun. One mile down this backwater, on right, is the entrance to Arun Canal (disused) which led through Hardham Tunnel and Waltham Lock to Arun 2 miles above Amberley.
$19\frac{5}{8}$	River Arun Junc.	

River Rother: extract from the *Oarsman's Guide*, 1896.

Pleasure skiffs passing through the remains of Shopham Lock in the summer of 1895.

place for artists and had a room with painted panels. Stopham Lock cut was blocked by felled trees – 'probably only temporarily'.

Although the Arun Navigation Company had presented a petition to wind up the concern in June 1888, Mr Justice North had declined to grant the order and it was not until the Board of Trade had held an inquiry, and disagreements between the various riparian landowners had been settled, that the warrant was formally issued authorizing the abandonment of the Arun Navigation in September 1896.[102]

In 1898 the London, Brighton & South Coast Railway, foreseeing the possibility of subsidence, decided to block up Hardham Tunnel at the points where it was crossed by the lines from Pulborough to Arundel and Petworth. This was not a simple operation. First a shaft several feet in circumference had to be bored a few feet from the main line and carried down 10 ft to the crown of the tunnel, which was pierced; thereupon tons of chalk and gravel were conveyed to the spot in trucks, tipped down the hole, and thrown up on either side to touch the roof of the tunnel immediately beneath both lines.[103] So were brought to a close the boating parties and river expeditions that had found the tunnel an intriguing site of exploration during the 1890s.

Maintenance of the Rother Navigation had ceased with the demise of barge traffic. Rushes and water-lilies soon choked the cuts; shoals and sandbanks formed in the river; lock-gates became unworkable and the navigation fell into disuetude. However, as many moribund canal and railway companies in the nineteenth century discovered, liabilities to riparian or adjoining landowners and to the public continued until such time as the powers granted under the original Act of Parliament had been abrogated. Of this fact Lord Leconfield was either unaware or unconcerned.

It had taken the Arun Navigation Company eight frustrating years to obtain its warrant of abandonment and it appears that as his lordship considered his navigation to be but a continuation of the Arun Navigation, the latter's closure in 1888 absolved him of further responsibility. In this he was wrong, and particularly for that part of the waterway which did not pass through his estate. The consequence of this omission to legally close the navigation was a nasty lawsuit.

In 1843 the 6th Earl of Egmont, an admiral on the reserve list who had distinguished himself at the battle of Navarino, had bought the Cowdray Estate for £300,000 from the three heiresses of William Poyntz who had died in 1840.[104] On the earl's death in 1874 the property had passed to his nephew Charles George Perceval. Shortly after barge traffic had ceased, the bank by Todham Lock, which formed part of the Cowdray Estate, had collapsed. Lord Egmont suggested that Lord Leconfield should pay the cost of repair, but the latter stated that he felt he was under no obligation to do so. An agreement was subsequently reached in June 1889 under which Leconfield undertook to repair the bank and place a floodgate at the upper end of the lock on the understanding that Egmont paid half the cost up to £50. Egmont also agreed to maintain the floodgate and was granted the right to remove any shoals above the lock. This agreement met the immediate problem but it made no provision for the future maintenance of the upper reaches.★

Now it so happened that after the heavy rains and floods of January 1903, the sluice gates of Todham Lock were torn asunder and the weir broken. Lord Leconfield saw no advantage to be gained in rebuilding the weir, so his men pulled down the remaining brickwork and allowed the river to revert to its natural, pre-1790, state. As a result the water level fell at least 2 ft.

It was perhaps unfortunate that this particular lock and weir should have been the one which still served a useful purpose in providing the owners of the Cowdray Park Estate with facilities for both angling and boating as well as an effectual ha-ha against cattle. The 7th earl had died in 1897 and his kinsman, who had succeeded to the title, found the mud exposed by the lower water level very offensive. Correspondence between the solicitors of the

---

★ The *Oarsman's Guide* reported in 1894 that the lower gates of the lock had been removed and that the upper were converted into sluice gates.

The remains of Todham Lock, 1994.

respective parties settled nothing. Consequently, in May 1903 Augustus Arthur, the 8th Earl of Egmont, issued a writ against Lord Leconfield claiming damages and seeking an injunction with costs. Leconfield defended the action which was heard in the High Court before Mr Justice Farwell. The defendant denied the allegations and claimed that he was not required under the provisions of the 1791 Navigation Act to raise or maintain the level of the river and that in any case 'both the river Arun and the river Rother have for upwards of twenty years past been disused for navigation'.[105]

The dispute was only resolved by both peers reaching a formal agreement, that as the navigation was now 'useless, owing to diversion of traffic and other causes' and that as some of the works were in decay (particularly part of the left bank above Todham Lock which had given way):

Lord Leconfield would within 3 months repair the bank above Todham Lock and place a floodgate at the upper end of the lock;
Lord Egmont would pay up to £50 towards the expense of this work;
Lord Egmont would have care and control of the sluices of the new floodgate and be responsible for its maintenance;

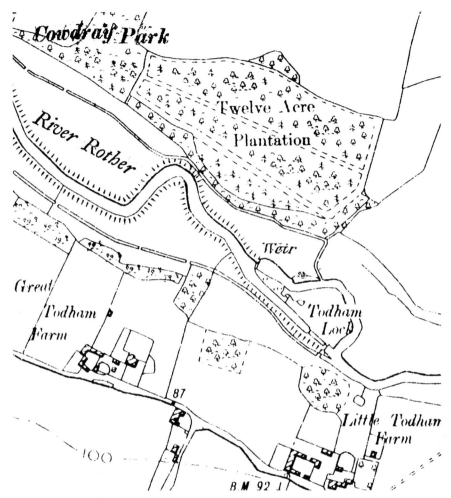

Todham Lock, 1895.

Lord Leconfield should have the right, after giving 3 days' notice, to draw
  the sluice;

Lord Leconfield would authorize Lord Egmont to exercise those rights
  empowered on him as owner of the navigation to dredge the river above
  Todham Lock;

Lord Egmont would indemnify Lord Leconfield for all claims arising out of
  this authority on the erection of the floodgates.

In 1906 Hilaire Belloc regretted that the canal system by which the Arun was linked up with the rest of England had been deliberately allowed to go to pieces and recalled that the Rother was 'canalised and usable for traffic until like all the rest of our waterways, it was killed by the railroads'. His plea for their resuscitation, however, was less than shrill as he refused to allow his name to be printed as the author of A. & C. Black's colour book on Sussex.

P. Bonthron, who cruised on some 2,000 miles of the canals and rivers of Great Britain in motor boat and skiff over a span of thirty years (1885–1915) described a trip on the Rother and Arun before the First World War.[106] What turned out to be 'a surprisingly delightful trip' took place before 1908.*

This is one of the most charming little rivers for its size one could find, and all along the valley one comes through varied picturesque views, showing beautiful, well-wooded scenery. The weather, too, being very fine after a spell of sunless days, made us appreciate everything all the more. The waterway tourist has the novel advantage of seeing the country from the river point of view as he passes along; a unique advantage and one which is consequently the privilege of the few.

We trained to Midhurst on the London, Brighton & South Coast Railway late in the afternoon to find our boat awaiting us, as previously arranged. This we procured from Mr Port, the local boatman (see page 141), and, strangely enough, in all his experience of some ten years back, he had never let a boat for such a through journey, although we did hear of one crew that came upstream, so the Rother is left severely alone in this respect.

Bonthron related how the disused locks entailed 'very heavy and troublesome portages' extending to 50 yards or more and how the various shallows and small weirs made voyaging hard work, but 'all this made a variety in the day's pleasure'. At Moorland Lock,

had we not had the kindly assistance of two young farmers (whose residence was close by), who accompanied us a part of the way giving further help, we should have had some trouble getting along. Moreover, our crew was one short, 'our ship's surgeon' having lost the train and missed his connection with the party. This brought the fact home that in doing the Rother two things are necessary, and these are a light boat and a full crew.

The only other obstacle we came across so far was a floating bridge at

---

* Bonthron mentions Littlehampton ferry and adds 'a bridge is now available'. The swing bridge was opened on 27 May 1908.

Rotherbridge Farmhouse and the site of Rotherbridge, pulled down in 1800. The bridge was replaced in the 1890s by Kelsham Floating Bridge, a curious structure used as a foot-bridge which, Bonthron noted on his trip down the Rother, could be opened by raising one end. This view was taken about 1925 and the bridge was replaced by a fixed suspension bridge in 1935 and by an iron bridge with tubular railings in 1961.

Kelsham, a mile from our stopping place. This can be opened by raising up one end, but we just lifted the boat over the platform.

Shortly after this we came to Coultershaw Lock, just adjacent to Petworth station, and here we moored our craft for the night, under the bridge at the mill; then proceeded to the town of Petworth, itself some 1½ miles from the lock. We were very comfortably accommodated at the Swan Hotel, and ready we were for our late supper after our exertions.

We came across several persons who remembered the time when the navigation was carried right up to Midhurst from Littlehampton. We also heard of an Oxford rowing man who at one time pulled from Oxford, via Godalming and the Wey & Arun Canal and Stopham Lock, to Midhurst.

The next morning remained fine. 'The river from here is very tortuous and wants careful steering, besides which we had to avoid the overhanging branches across the river.' After stopping at Fittleworth to visit the Artist's Room in the Swan Hotel and to admire the signboard painted by R. Caton

View of Fittleworth Mill. The navigation channel at left is leading to the lock, 1895.

The derelict lower gates of Fittleworth Lock viewed in August 1899.

The Artist's Room, Swan Hotel, Fittleworth, 1914. The room is still used by hotel guests.

Woodville, they proceeded to Stopham Lock which involved another severe portage – the seventh in all. All in all, due to the various navigational hazards, it took about eight hours to scull the dozen miles to the Arun. At Pulborough they lunched at the Swan before going on down to Arundel and putting up at the Bridge Hotel. At this point their skiff was railed back to Midhurst while they chartered a small motor boat to take them down to Littlehampton.

Returning to Pulborough by train from Arundel, they chartered a skiff from Sam Strudwick ('whose father had done service on both the Rother Navigation and Portsmouth & Arundel Canal') and proceeded to Pallingham Quay, where they left their boat and continued along the tow-path of the derelict Arun Canal to Newbridge. Bonthron recalled that 'our walk along the bank was such that to us it seemed to open up a new source of pleasure by traversing the disused canals in England with their unfrequented routes and scenes'; and another thing, too, one is practically always walking on 'the level'.

A more unusual account of a five-day canoe voyage appeared in Eleanor Barnes's record of adventures in a canoe on the rivers and trout streams of southern England.[107] One December, in 1913 or 1914, she spent five days with a girlfriend called Sabrina, descending the Arun and the Rother. It was an enjoyable trip in spite of various hazards 'and more and more we were convinced of the chill beauty, nay, the joy, and wisdom of a winter expedition'.

Their minimum necessities constituted toothbrushes, comb, silk night-dress, a thin change of costume, galoshes, rubber mackintosh, milk flask, thermos and two books, all contained in a knapsack. The canoe 'of lightest frailest build' was made of green plywood and canvas and weighed 30 lb. After canoeing from Newbridge to Stopham in two days, they hired a cart and from Midhurst paddled back down the river. No mention was made of the canal basin nor of Port's boathouse, which had been burnt down around 1912.

At Moorland Farm Lock they nearly met disaster:

Now on the Rother we were nearly drowned. It has been said we came near death a score of times by reason of fierce landlords, anglers, bulls, barbed wire, low bridges, shallows, hunger, cold and fear, but only once 'tis true, and in this wise.

We always questioned those we met upon the bank, partly because we met so few, partly because Sabrina when excited likes to raise her gentle voice and shout.

I can't suppose we raised these questionings hoping for information, that would assume an optimism too abnormal, even for ourselves.

The occasional angler proved invariably unacquainted with the river's

Moorland Lock drawn by Helen Stratton, *c.* 1913.

course, except that isolated spot on which he stood, but ever he refused confession of his ignorance, and when he cried with confidence, 'Proceed, there's no impediment,' we always met with wire and waterfalls, but if he warned us to beware upon our lives, we smiled and paddled on, learning mistrust of all his foolish words.

Now on this day of danger we gave greeting to a fisherman, Sabrina asking if there were a mill or fall below the river's bend.

He shouted back, 'It is a dangerous place, get out and walk, or you will soon be drowned.'

Moorland Lock in 1994.

We eyed him critically, then pulled the boat on to the bank, walking some distance, but the stream pursued its placid course.

Returning, with some irritation we embarked again, and paddled on about a mile.

Then suddenly, without visible sign of any such development, the current, flowing softly on the surface, became exceedingly swift. The boat raced forward, but Sabrina, stretching her long arm towards the shore, caught at an alder twig, which mercifully held. The turbid water now rushed past us silently, and as we held the green one straight, and fast against the bank, the swiftness was so great, I feared the flood would overflow the shallow freeboard of the boat.

Leaping ashore, we found behind some shrunken posts a broken lock [Moorland], and the full river, shooting smoothly from above, fell into angry foam a dozen feet below. And underneath the fall a rustic fixed his stolid gaze upon a fishing line. He looked up sullenly as I approached, pulling the boat behind me, followed by Sabrina carrying knapsacks, mackintoshes, books and food.

'We nearly paddled over there just now,' I told him, pointing at the fall.

He stared at me indifferently, then at the foaming lock. After a heavy pause he answered: 'Did yer now?' and re-arranged his worm.

Our merciful escape seemed less momentous after his remark, and we proceeded, though with considerable caution.

Shopham lock posed no problem:

One fairy bend branched, with swift, rippling water, through a bower of overhanging trees, but we refused the looping turn, kept a straight course, and shooting down some rapids, met the stream again.

These little falls occur midst pastoral scene of never failing grace, and every one is christened by the rustics 'Tumble Bay'.

That night in dream I saw the stolid angler's face, Sabrina, and the green one, paddles, knapsack, books, mackintoshes, riding upon the flood, tossed in chaotic unconvention in the pool which whirled about his feet, and half awake, I laughed so much, Sabrina grumbled – in her sleep.

As the Water Flows was first published by Grant Richards in 1920 and reprinted by Clement Ingleby in 1927. The book contains a charming colour drawing by Helen Stratton entitled *Dream* illustrating the fate that might have overtaken them at Moorland Lock. In 1922 Eleanor Barnes became the second wife of the distinguished eighty-year-old marine engineer and shipbuilder Sir Alfred Yarrow (1842–1932), but she had known him for many years previously as a family friend. 'My Guardian Gabriel' is how she refers to him throughout the book.

Sir Alfred Yarrow had married the beautiful Minnie Franklin in 1875;[108] she bore him six children but the partnership did not work smoothly. In 1903, after his daughters were married, his mother's great friend and his own 'most valued adviser' Mrs Barnes, then ninety years of age, went to live with him, accompanied by her granddaughter Eleanor. On her deathbed two years later she requested that Eleanor should remain to care for the welfare of one who was as dear to her as a son. After seven years without a break (1905–12), Eleanor Barnes found the strain beginning to tell. She secretly bought an old canoe, but was discovered by Sir Alfred trying it out in wintry weather on a nearby loch. Finally she wrested from him five days leave in every hundred. In 1913 they decided to leave Scotland to live in the south and Eleanor Barnes's canoeing adventures began. For the next seven or eight years she and a friend canoed down the trout streams and rivers of southern England – the chapter entitled 'Forgive us our trespasses' indicating that her passage down the River Anton from her home at Lower Clatford to the Test must have caused some anguish to her fly-fishing friends. Lady Yarrow died in Dublin in 1953.

The *Reliance* of Fittleworth moored above Stopham Bridge in 1905, with bargemaster Sam Strudwick and Loyal Saigeman. The barge was 72 ft × 12 ft.

After the closure of the Rother Navigation, John Strudwick (1821–1903) moved the *Eleanor* down from Fittleworth to Pulborough, where he and fellow bargemaster Henry Doick (1847–1902) continued to work the Arun. Doick, who owned a third share of no. 64, made in the space of seven years (1895–1901) 521 voyages up and down the Arun carrying 17,096 tons of cargo between Littlehampton and Pulborough. Gross earnings averaged £163 p.a.; the average load weighed 33 tons, the maximum 38; the principal consignments were chalk, coal, culm, gravel and sand, but from time to time Doick carried ballast for Littlehampton brigs, steam coal for Arundel, bolts of reeds and osiers for Pepper & Son at Houghton, gas coal to Greatham and flints for the Duke of Norfolk at Timberley and for the rector of Pulborough. Additional earnings arose from pile driving, and usually once or twice a year no. 64 was hired out to Mr Slaughter of York House School, Brighton, for barge parties to the Black Rabbit pub and picnics in South Woods. Doick delivered a barge-load of coal to Greatham Wharf on 19 April 1902. It was to be his last; six months later he died at the age of fifty-five. For thirty years he had been one of the bell-ringers at Pulborough Church. The rector, churchwardens and bell-ringers erected and inscribed his tombstone 'as a mark of their respect and esteem'.[109]

Bargemaster John Strudwick died six weeks later aged eighty-two. In his will, dated 3 December 1888, he bequeathed his furniture and one cow to his wife and the remainder of his livestock, his house and his ageing barge *Eleanor* to his son Sam (1864–1933), who replaced her with the *Reliance* in 1905. It was about this time that traffic above Stopham Bridge ceased with the closing of the brickworks at Harwoods Green. For eighteen years the *Reliance* operated between Pulborough and Arundel. In 1923, however, Strudwick sold her to the Arun Brick Company. This company had speculated in a clay pit at Rackham with the idea of building a light railway to Greatham Wharf. Strudwick's work with the company lasted little more than a year before it failed, and in July 1925 the harbourmaster at Littlehampton reported that the brick company had agreed to give the abandoned *Reliance* to the commissioners in return for its removal from the tideway.[110]

Whereas both the Wey & Arun Navigations had been officially abandoned, the Rother Navigation was still legally a public right of way. Roger Sellman, then an Oxford undergraduate who had been researching the history of the waterways of Sussex, drew attention to this fact. Technically, anyone could come along with a boat, offer the proper toll dues, and wait for the owners to rebuild the locks and put the navigation in order. Consequently the Petworth and Cowdray estates were prompted to regularize the matter. For instance, if the Midhurst brickworks with its considerable output had suddenly decided to use water transport, a situation similar to that which arose when the Kennet & Avon Canal became semi-derelict in the 1950s might have arisen.* The Petworth and Cowdray estates therefore applied to the Minister of Transport for a warrant to authorize the abandonment of the navigation under section 45 of the Railway & Canal Traffic Act 1888 on the grounds that it was unnecessary for the purposes of public navigation.

It appears almost inevitable that as soon as a public announcement is made

---

* At a hearing before Mr Justice Roxburgh in the Chancery Division of the High Court in 1955, a canal carrier sought an injunction to restrain the British Transport Commission, the then owners of the Kennet & Avon Canal, from causing further deterioration to the waterway. In the course of the proceedings Sir Andrew Clark for the defendants asked: 'Is it right to spend hundreds of thousands of pounds on a canal merely because one man wants to sail a couple of boats on it?' His lordship's answer to that proposition was if that was the law, then it was the duty of a statutory monopoly to obey it, just as much as any one else.

RIVER ROTHER NAVIGATION.

On the matter of the Railway and Canal Traffic Act, 1888. and an application by the Right Honourable Charles Henry Baron Leconfield, G.C.V.O., and the Cowdray Trust Limited and John Lister Walsh (as Trustees of the Cowdray Estate, Sussex) for a Warrant authorising the abandonment of the River Rother Navigation.

NOTICE IS HEREBY GIVEN that by a Warrant dated the fifteenth day of April, One thousand nine hundred and thirty six under the Seal of the Minister of Transport the Minister authorised the abandonment of the Right Honourable Charles Henry Baron Leconfield, G.C.V.O., and the Cowdray Trust limited and John Lister Walsh (as Trustees of the Cowdray Estate, Sussex) of the River Rother Navigation.

Dated this 29th day of April, 1936.

FARRER & CO.,
66, Lincoln's Inn Fields, W.C. 2.
(Solicitors for Lord Leconfield)
MARKBY STEWART & WADESONS,
5, Bishopsgate, E.C. 2.
(Solicitors for The Cowdray Trust Limited and J. L. Walsh Esquire).

West Sussex Gazette,
16 May 1936.

of an intention to legalize a situation, which everyone has hitherto accepted without protest, objections are sure to be received. On this occasion objections were lodged by the River Arun Catchment Board, on the grounds that the efficiency of the river as a drainage channel might be affected, and from a local canoe club.[111] However, on 15 April 1936 the warrant was granted, and so, as had happened with the Portsmouth & Arundel Canal, some fifty years after the last boat had passed through, the obituary of the Rother Navigation was published in a local newspaper.[112]

EPILOGUE

It is two hundred years since the first barge brought coal to Midhurst Wharf and a century has now passed since the locks on the Rother Navigation were allowed to fall into disuse. All over the kingdom a similar fate befell many famous waterways. From time to time boating enthusiasts have bewailed the loss of a facility, but not until the 1960s did dreams turn themselves into deeds with the formation of voluntary trusts to do the work.

The Rother Navigation remains one of the few English waterways to remain unadopted by any restoration society. Most of the canals in southern England, like the Basingstoke, Kennet & Avon, Chichester and Wey & Arun Junction, have well-established organizations pledged to their restoration. The Rother deserves such attention. Its reopening for small pleasure boats would add to the enjoyment of exploring the tidal Arun. If the riparian owners and the National Rivers Authority would agree to allow a right of passage, voluntary labour could be recruited to excavate the silted entrance channel at Stopham and to build rollers to assist boats through or around the existing lock chambers, all of which remain *in situ* although that at Lodsbridge now serves as a swimming pool. The total sum required to reopen the navigation to Midhurst would be small compared to the cost of reopening a 12-mile canal.

Appendices

1. Table of Locks and Distances on the Rother Navigation and its Links with the Thames and the English Channel 1820

The distances on the Rother Navigation are those used by the toll collector at Fittleworth.

Navigation	Lock	Place	Distance (miles furlongs)		Distance from River Arun (miles furlongs)	
Rother	From	Junction River Arun to:				
(12 miles)	1	Stopham	0	1		
	2	Fittleworth	1	3	1	4
		Coates Wharf	1	4	3	0
		Shopham Wharf	0	4	3	4
	3	Shopham	0	4	4	0
		Junction Petworth Canal	0	2	4	2
		Coultershaw Wharf	0	4	4	6
	4	Coultershaw	0	$0\frac{1}{2}$	4	$6\frac{1}{2}$
		Rotherbridge Wharf	0	$7\frac{1}{2}$	5	6
	5	Ladymead	2	0	7	6
	6	Lodsbridge	1	0	8	6
	7	Moorland	0	4	9	2
		Ambersham Wharf	0	6	10	0
	8	Todham	0	2	10	2
		Poyntzs' Wharf	0	6	11	0
		Midhurst Basin	1	0	12	0
Petworth Canal	From	Junction Rother Navigation to:				
($1\frac{1}{4}$ miles)	1	Hains	0	4	4	6
	2	Upper Lock	0	$3\frac{1}{2}$	5	$1\frac{1}{2}$
		Haslingbourne Wharf	0	$4\frac{1}{2}$	5	6

SUMMARY OF DISTANCES

From Midhurst down to:	Shortest Distance (miles)	No. of Locks	From Midhurst up to:	Shortest Distance (miles)	No. of Locks
Petworth	7	5	Pallingham Quay	14½	8
Fittleworth	10½	7	Newbridge	19	11
Pulborough	13	8	Loxwood	25	16
Greatham Bridge	16½	8	Bramley	36	32
Bury Wharf	17	11	Godalming	39½	36
Houghton Bridge	18	11	Guildford	39½	36
Arundel	24½	11	Aldershot	69½	73
Littlehampton	31½	11	Basingstoke	88½	73
Chichester	39½	13	Weybridge	54	46
Portsmouth	55½	17	London Bridge	85	51

Note: See also Appendix B in *London's Lost Route to the Sea* for details of the locks between London Bridge and Portsmouth. The minimum draught throughout was 3 ft 1 in; the minimum headroom 7 ft. The length of Hardham Tunnel was 375 yards.

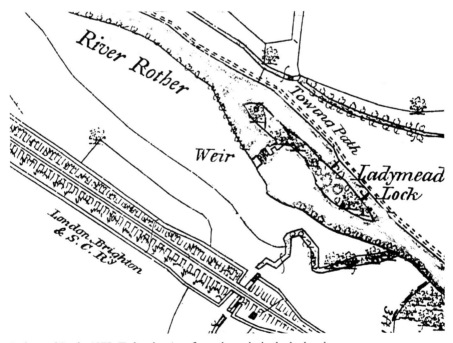

Ladymead Lock, 1875. Today the river flows through the lock chamber.

2. Proprietors, Officers and Servants of the Rother Navigation

Proprietor

1791–1837 3rd Earl of Egremont
1837–1869 Col. George Wyndham
  (created 1st Lord Leconfield 1859)
1869–1901 2nd Lord Leconfield
1901–1936 3rd Lord Leconfield

Clerk / Attorney / Steward

1791–1794 James Upton
1794–1801 James Upton Tripp

1801–1835 William Tyler
1835–1847 Charles Murray
1847–1854 James Murray
1854–1865 J.M. Brydone
1866–1874 Henry Brydone
1874–1879 William Ingram

Superintendent

1791–1837(?) Thomas Poling Upton
1837(?)–1840 Henry Upton I
1840–1874(?) Henry Upton II

Collector of Tolls & Lock-keeper
at Fittleworth

1793–1819 John King I
1819–1820 Mary King
1820–1840 John King II
1841–1874(?) Anthony Whitting

Wharfingers

Coultershaw
1793–1837 Uncertain
1838 Robert Dearling
1841 James Hooker
1841–1869 John Stoner
1870–1874(?) Hampson Ireland

Midhurst
1795–1819 William Smith
1820–1832 William Goodner
1832–1855 John Smart
1855–1874(?) James Grist

3. ROTHER NAVIGATION TRAFFIC RECEIPTS (1793–1888)

Year	Tolls(£)	Estimated Tonnage	Year	Tolls(£)	Estimated Tonnage
1793	250★	2,800	1831	1,030	11,680
1794	475★	5,500	1832	944	11,800
1795	355	4,000	1833	929	11,500
1796	544	6,100	1834	1,000	12,500
1797	339	3,750	1835	872	11,000
1798	262	3,000	1836	1,007	12,500
1799	326	3,500	1837	1,075★	13,500
1800	597	6,600	1838	1,087	13,500
1801	628	7,000	1839	1,302	16,000
1802	576	6,400	1840	1,079	13,500
1803	531	5,900	1841	1,148	14,250
1804	499	5,600	1842	970	13,350
1805	571	6,400	1843	1,026	12,627
1806	577★	6,400	1844	945	12,500
1807	817★	9,000	1845	1,150	15,000
1808	867★	9,500	1846	1,058	13,500
1809	719★	8,000	1847	986	13,000
1810	800★	8,800	1848–1854	Not known	
1811	700★	7,600	1855	894	12,000
1812	650★	7,100	1856	1,097	14,500
1813	1,100★	11,800	1857	1,231	16,500
1814	900★	9,200	1858	1,274	17,000
1815	1,245★	7,800	1859	1,024	13,500
1816	900	10,000	1860	1,015	13,500
1817	1,201	13,750	1861	1,182	15,500
1818	1,073	12,250	1862	1,231	16,500
1819	1,126	12,750	1863	967	13,000
1820	1,066	12,000	1864	608	8,000
1821	808	9,250	1865	535	7,000
1822	766	9,750	1866	429	5,750
1823	962	10,290	1867	413	5,500
1824	1,139	12,540	1868	367	5,000
1825	1,287	13,815	1869	490	6,500
1826	1,009	11,000	1870	302	4,000
1827	984	11,250	1871	301	4,000
1828	1,074	14,100	1872	198	2,750
1829	862	12,500	1873	166	3,250
1830	1,111	12,310	1874	142	2,750

★ Some months averaged.

Year	Tolls (£)	Estimated Tonnage	Year	Tolls (£)	Estimated Tonnage
1875	163	3,250	1881	92	2,500
1876	134	2,750	1882	63	2,000
1877	140	2,750	1883	86	2,750
1878	120	3,200	1884	48	1,600
1879	97	2,500	1885–1888	Not known	
1880	111	3,000			

Note: Tolls were only collected at Fittleworth. Additional revenue arose from wharfage dues at Petworth and Midhurst. No tolls were payable between Stopham and Arundel unless the short cut was taken through Hardham Tunnel. The toll of 1s a ton was payable to the Arun Navigation Company whose traffic returns will be found listed in *London's Lost Route to the Sea*, Appendix D.

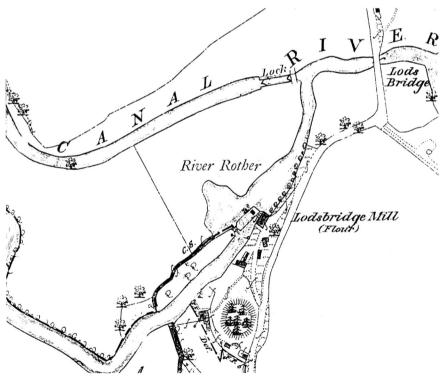

Lodsbridge, Selham, 1875.

4. ANALYSIS OF BARGE TRAFFIC ON THE ROTHER NAVIGATION IN 1843
(535 tickets issued)

Bargemaster	Of	No. of Barges★	No. of loads			Tonnage Carried			Principal Cargoes
			Up	Down	Total	Up Westward	Down Eastward	Total	
Barnett		1	–	2	2	–	50	50	Hoops
Bonamy, Thomas	Arundel	4	41	21	62	349½	273½	623	Groceries, hoops, bark, wheat
Boxall, Henry	Lodsbridge	1	5	–	5	128	–	128	Culm
Bridger	Petworth	4	2	8	10	46	206¾	252¾	timber
Chatfield		1	15	1	16	394½	8	402½	Chalk, culm
Clue, John		5	38	18	56	908½	501	1,409½	Coal, culm, chalk, groceries, seaweed, timber
Cooper, James	Houghton	1	21	–	21	350	–	350	Bricks
Evershed, Samuel	Arundel	2	52	14	66	1,399½	213¾	1,613¼	Coal, chalk, sand, slate, timber
Fry, Thomas	Arundel	2	1	2	3	8½	14	22½	Coal, timber
Goatcher, Richard	Petworth	2	37	3	40	1,316	108	1,424	Coal, culm, stone, timber
Henly, John	Bury	7	16	3	19	311	28	339	Coal, lime, seaweed
Hubard		1	1	–	1	17	–	17	Chalk
King, John	Fittleworth	2	–	10	10	–	189	189	Hoops, timber
Lawson		1	4	8	12	65	190¾	255¾	Coal, timber, seaweed
Leman		2	5	11	16	160	288	448	Coal, sand
Man		1	–	2	2	–	22	22	Hoops
Peacock, John	Arundel	1	4	–	4	115	–	115	Coal
Pewtress, Benjamin	Iping	2	24	6	30	666½	156¾	823¼	Coal, hoops, paper, wheat
Sharp, George		1	1	–	1	12	–	12	Bricks
Smart, Richard, William & John	Houghton Arundel &	6	26	9	35	774	243	1,017	Coal, bark, timber, seaweed
Smith	Midhurst	1	1	–	1	14	–	14	Slate
Stanton, James	Bramley	3	1	7	8	18	178¾	196¾	Bark, hoops
Stoveld William (dcd)	Petworth	1	4	1	5	88	11¼	99¼	Seaweed, coal
Wackford Edmund	Petworth	1	8	–	8	131½	–	131½	Coal
Warren, William	Pulborough	3	97	2	99	2,530	57	2,587	Chalk, culm, lime manure
West		1	3	–	3	85	–	85	Coal
TOTAL		57★	407	128	535	9,887½	2,739½	12,627	

★ licensed to operate on the Rother Navigation.

SUMMARY OF CARGOES

	Tonnage Carried		
	Up	*Down*	*Total*
Coal	5,301		5,301
Timber		1,831	1,831
Hoops		340	340
Groceries	408		408
Chalk	2,280		2,280
Seaweed	464		464
Miscellaneous	1,434½	568½	2,003
TOTAL	9,887½	2,739½	12,627 tons

5. COMPARATIVE TOLLS AND TONNAGES 1790–1880

Tolls (£):

Year	Wey Navigation	Wey & Arun Canal	Arun Navigation	Rother Navigation
1790	4,236	–	376	–
1795	4,750	–	914	355
1800	5,860	–	1,000★	597
1810	6,000★	–	1,050★	800★
1820	5,678	1,343	1,350★	1,066
1830	5,571	2,181	1,300	1,111
1839	7,642	2,524	2,426	1,302
1840	6,881	2,189	2,407	1,079
1850	3,173	1,036	1,460	1,000★
1860	3,001	787	1,020	1,015
1870	2,083	278	497	302
1880	1,549	–	152	111

Tonnages:

Year	Wey Navigation	Wey & Arun Canal	Arun Navigation	Rother Navigation
1790	32,981	–	6,500★	–
1795	35,500★	–	15,000★	4,000★
1800	57,500	–	17,000★	6,600★
1810	68,500★	–	17,600★	8,800★
1820	56,400	9,000★	20,000★	12,000★
1830	55,035	17,500★	20,000★	12,310
1839	78,878	23,250★	36,000★	16,000★
1840	75,990	20,500★	36,000★	13,500★
1850	47,250	15,121	29,000★	13,000★
1860	60,707	15,750★	20,000★	13,500★
1870	41,585	5,500★	10,000★	4,000★
1880	29,414	–	6,000★	3,000★

★ estimated.

6. Original Shareholders in the Arun Navigation Company

Share Capital £10,000 in £100 shares

Date	Name	No. of shares subscribed
1785	Sir Harry Goring	10
1785	John Cutfield – Clymping	10
1785	Daniel Digance – Arundel	10
1785	Henry Digance – Arundel	10
1785	Thomas Hampton	10
1785	Richard Smart	3
1785	Edward Carleton	2
1785	Revd Michael Dorset – Walberton	2
1785	William Hills	2
1785	Henry Napper	2
1785	Joseph Sanders the younger	2
1785	William Sandham	2
1785	Thomas Seward	2
1785	William Tate	2
1785	John King	1
1793	Executors Henry Digance	2
1793	Thomas Seward	2
1796	Earl of Egremont – Petworth	26

Note: In 1796 Lord Egremont subscribed for the balance of shares authorized by the Act and also purchased the holding of Sir Harry Goring.

NOTES

Abbreviations

ESRO   East Sussex Record Office
HL   House of Lords
PHA   Petworth House Archives
PRO   Public Record Office
SAC   *Sussex Archaeological Collections*
SNQ   Sussex Notes and Queries

1. Robert H. Goodsell, *The Arun and Western Rother*, 1962, describes the rivers in detail.
2. E. Jervoise, *The Ancient Bridges of the South of England,* 1930, pp. 54–5.
3. Quoted by Mary Maxse, *The Story of Fittleworth*, 1935, p. 50.
4. William Jessop, report on the Rother Navigation – 16 April 1783 (PHA O.F. 13/12).
5. Henry Digance, *Thoughts of the great Advantages arising from Inland Navigation in General . . .* (? Arundel, 1783).
6. See Charles Hadfield & A.W. Skempton, *William Jessop, Engineer*, 1979. It is surprising that Jessop is not listed in the *Dictionary of National Biography*.
7. Standing Orders of the House of Commons – Navigable Canals, Aqueducts and the navigation of Rivers – 7 May 1794.
8. The Creevey Papers (Thomas Creevey MP 1768–1838), 6 November 1820.
9. R. Hyam and G. Martin, *Reappraisals in British Imperial History*, 1975, p. 27.
10. Holland House Mss quoted by H.A. Wyndham, 'A Family History', Vol. II, pp. 217–18.
11. *ibid.*, p. 219.
12. *ibid.*, p. 220.
13. Creevey's *Life and Times*, 1828, p. 276.
14. *Lady Bessborough and her Family Circle*, ed. Earl of Bessborough, 1940, p. 474.
15. C.R. Leslie, *Autobiographical Recollections*, 1860.
16. *The Greville Memoirs 1814–1860*, 1938, Vol. III, p. 398.
17. Revd Arthur Young, *General View of the Agriculture of the County of Sussex*, 1808, pp. 188–9.
18. William Marshall, *The Rural Economy of the Southern Counties*, 1794.
19. 'Nimrod' (C. Apperley), *The Chace, the Turf and the Road*, new edition, 1870, p. 147.
20. Roger Mortimer, *The History of the Derby Stakes*, 1962, p. 29.
21. Ms., 15 June 1793 (PHA 91).
22. John Farrant, 'The Arthur Youngs and the Board of Agriculture's Reports on Sussex, 1793 and 1808', *SAC* Vol. 130, 1992, p. 205.
23. M. Betham-Edwardes (ed.), *The Autobiography of Arthur Young*, 1898, p. 313.
24. Letter postmarked 6 October 1800, quoted in 'Turner of Petworth', p. 107 (PHA 91).
25. Revd Young, p. 380.

26. *ibid.*, p. 363.
27. Diary of Joseph Farington, Vol. II, 27 March 1804.
28. Revd Young, p. 141.
29. *ibid.*, p. 58.
30. Letter Book London, 6 April 1790 (Institution of Civil Engineers).
31. Ms., Thomas Upton to John King, Wharfinger at Fittleworth, 21 May 1817 (PHA).
32. Ms., Thomas Upton to Lord Egremont, 26 June 1832 (PHA).
33. Graham Reynolds, *The Later Paintings and Drawings of John Constable*, 1984, text p. 262.
34. *The Journal of the Hon. Henry Edward Fox, afterward the fourth and last Lord Holland, 1818–1830*, 1923, p. 183.
35. E.B. George, *The Life and Death of Benjamin Robert Haydon (1786–1846)*, 1948, p. 184.
36. William Cobbett also makes reference to haymaking and stone cracking (*Rural Rides*, Vol. I, Journal entry, 1 August 1823).
37. *The Greville Diary*, ed. P.W. Wilson, 1927, Vol. I, pp. 469–70.
38. Revd Young, p. 383.
39. *The Greville Diary*, Vol. I, p. 469.
40. *The Creevey Papers*, 1903, Ch. VI, p. 164.
41. SAC, Vol. XCV, 1957, p. 111.
42. Revd Young, pp. 426–7.
43. Ms., William Jessop to Lord Sheffield, October 1790 (ESRO).
44. See also Hadfield and Skempton, p. 37.
45. P.A.L. Vine, *London's Lost Route to Basingstoke*, 1994, p. 22.
46. Basingstoke Canal Navigation Company Report, 2 November 1789.
47. Jones v. Corporation of Proprietors of the Thames & Severn Canal Navigation, Hilary Term, 21 March 1795 (PRO C.33/488, p. 285d). The bill in Chancery was filed in 1792.
48. Humphrey Household, *The Thames & Severn Canal*, 1969, pp. 55–61.
49. Revd Young, p. 406.
50. Ms., William Jessop to Lord Sheffield, 6 December 1791 (ESRO).
51. PHA F13/16a.
52. Revd Gilbert White, 'The Natural History of Selborne, and the naturalist's Calendar' (Meteorological Observations), 1802.
53. Ms., Jessop to Sheffield, 3 September 1792 (ESRO).
54. Grand Junction Canal Minute Book, 11 December 1793, quoted by Hadfield & Skempton.
55. Grand Junction Lower District Committee Minute Book, 20 May 1794, quoted by Alan Faulkner in *The Grand Junction Canal*, 1972.
56. Revd Stebbing Shaw, *A Tour to the West of England in 1788*, 1789, p. 545.
57. Rex v. Rowland Harper, April 1796 (PHA 6310).
58. PHA O.F. 13/15/1–20.
59. Ms., Newark, 23 November 1794 (PHA).
60. Revd Young, pp. 421–2.
61. This concession was approved at a meeting of the proprietors held on 7 December 1789. An Abstract of the Act of Parliament for the Arun Navigation for the Use of the Merchants, Owners of Barges and Workmen therein concerned together with such Bye

Laws and Rules as the Company have hitherto enacted for Good Government thereof, MDCCXC, pp. 4–5.

62. Quoted in P.A.L. Vine's *London's Lost Route to the Sea*, 1965, p. 141.
63. PHA O.F. 13/19/14.
64. Revd Young, p. 425.
65. Arun Navigation Minutes, December 1793.
66. *ibid.*, June 1796.
67. Quoted by H.A. Wyndham, *The Wyndham Family*, 1950, Vol. II, p. 333.
68. PHA O.F. 13/12.
69. Ms., 8 March 1793 (PHA O.F. 13/16 b).
70. Ms., J. Granger to George Stubbs, 21 July 1793. Granger also refers to the plan for a 55-mile canal from Petworth to Kingston-on-Thames via the Dorking Canal.
71. House of Lords petition, 28 February 1792, relating to Arun and Rother navigations.
72. Revd Young, p. 423.
73. PHA O.F. 13/16 b.
74. 'An Act to continue for Twenty-one Years and alter the powers of two Acts made in 1758 and 1765 for amending the roads from Milford through Petworth to top of Duncton Hill.'
75. *SAC*, 1957, Vol. 95, pp. 105–15. The turnpike was abolished on 1 May 1877.
76. Ms., T.P. Upton to J. King, 7 July 1817.
77. *The Times*, 19 September 1826.
78. The account books for the years 1792 to 1808 survive in the Petworth House Archives.
79. Ms., William Stoveld to William Tyler, 6 March 1819.
80. Revd Young, p. 436.
81. PHA F10/23/61.
82. Revd Young, p. 166.
83. Ms., William Jessop to Lord Egremont, 5 February 1795 (PHA F13/15/5).
84. PHA O.F. 13/16a.
85. Ms., Mitford to Tyler, 8 June 1809 (PHA F13/16a).
86. Revd Young, p. 469.
87. Ms., Thomas Upton to Lord Egremont, 26 June 1832 (PHA).
88. Mackail & Wyndham, *Life and Letters of George Wyndham*, n.d., *c.* 1920. Vol. I, p. 10.
89. Ms., 14 March 1844 to the commissioners of the Port of Arundel.
90. Guildford Muniment Room 1317, Box 16.
91. P. Bonthron, *My Holidays on Inland Waterways*, 1916, p. 65.
92. HL Wey & Arun Junction Canal (Abandonment) Bill, Minutes of Evidence, 25 March 1868, p. 39.
93. J.B. Dashwood, *The Thames to the Solent*, 1868, p. 44.
94. HL Minutes of Evidence, 25 March 1868, p. 37.
95. *ibid.*, pp. 31–2.
96. *ibid.*, p. 23.
97. *ibid.*, pp. 37 and 39.
98. Sketches of locks on the navigation, which appeared in the *Illustrated Sporting and Dramatic News* on 20 April and 15 June 1889, indicate that some were in disrepair and unworkable.

99. P.A.L. Vine's *Pleasure Boating in the Victorian Era*, 1983, describes many of these excursions.

100. The voyage is described in *London's Lost Route to the Sea*, Chapter XIII.

101. *The Story of Fittleworth*, 1935, pp. 90–1.

102. The problems which the Arun Navigation Company faced in obtaining the Warrant of Abandonment are detailed in *London's Lost Route to the Sea*, Chapter XV.

103. Letter from former Chief Clerk, Civil Engineers' Dept. (SR) Brighton, published *Sussex County Magazine*, May 1953.

104. W.H. St. John Hope, *Cowdray and Easebourne Priory*, 1919, p. 27.

105. Statement of Defence delivered 12 August 1903 by Milles, Jennings, White & Foster, solicitors for the defendant (PHA 13/42/2–3).

106. *My Holidays on Inland Waterways*, 1916, Chapter X.

107. *As The Water Flows*, 1920, pp. 58–71. Similar voyages were also made on the Avon, the Mole and the Dorsetshire and Kentish Stour.

108. Lady Yarrow, *Alfred Yarrow*, 1923, p. 42.

109. I am indebted to Dr Richard Pepper for this information.

110. Minutes of meeting of the commissioners of the Port of Arundel, 21 July 1925.

111. Ms., Gerald Randall to Roger Sellman, 16 May 1936.

112. *West Sussex Gazette*, 16 May 1936.

BIBLIOGRAPHY

(I) ACT OF PARLIAMENT

1791   An Act to enable the Earl of Egremont to make and maintain the River Rother navigable, from the town of Midhurst, to a certain Meadow called the Railed Pieces, or Stopham Meadow, in the parish of Stopham, and a navigable Cut from the said River to the River Arun, at or near Stopham Bridge, in the county of Sussex; and for other purposes. (Rother Navigation Act)

(II) BOOKS OF REFERENCE

1795	William Marshall, *The Rural Economy of the Southern Counties*.
1808	Revd Arthur Young, *A General View of the Agriculture of the County of Sussex*.
1815–32	James Dallaway, *A History of the Western Division of the County of Sussex*, 3 vols.
1826	William Cobbett, *Rural Rides*.
1831	J. Priestley, *Historical Account of the Navigable Rivers, Canals and Railways throughout Great Britain*.
1833	Lengths and Levels to Bradshaw's Maps of the Canals, Navigable Rivers and Railways.
1835	T.W. Horsfield, *The History, Antiquities and Topography of the County of Sussex*.
1837	'Nimrod' *The Chace, the Turf and the Road*, ill. Henry Alken.
1857	*The Oarsman's Guide to the Thames and Other Rivers* (2nd ed.).
1864	Revd T.H. Arnold, *Petworth: a sketch of its History and Antiquities*.
1865	Mark Anthony Lower, *The Worthies of Sussex*.
1868	J.B. Dashwood, *The Thames to the Solent by Canal and Sea*.
1896	F.E. Prothero & W.A. Clarke, *A New Oarsman's Guide to the Rivers and Canals of Great Britain and Ireland*.
1897	H.R. De Salis, *Chronology of Inland Navigation*.
1898	M. Betham-Edwardes (ed.), *The Autobiography of Arthur Young with Selections from his Correspondence*.
1903	Sir Herbert Maxwell (ed.), *The Creevey Papers*.
1912	A.S. Cooke, *Off the Beaten Track in Sussex*.
1916	P. Bonthron, *My Holidays on Inland Waterways*.
1920	Eleanor Barnes, *As the Water Flows*.
1927	P.W. Wilson (ed.), *The Greville Diary*.
1929	Anon., *The High Stream of Arundel*. Written *c.* 1637. Edited J. Fowler.
1930	Hadrian A. Allcroft, *Waters of Arun*.
1935	Lady Maxse, *Story of Fittleworth*.

1950   H.A. Wyndham, *A Family History 1688–1837.*
1962   R.H. Goodsall, *The Arun and Western Rother.*
1965   P.A.L. Vine, *London's Lost Route to the Sea.*
1968–79   F.W. Steer, N.H. Osborne & T. McCann (eds) *The Petworth House Archives*, 2 vols.
1969   Charles Hadfield, *The Canals of South and South East England.*
1976   P.A. Jerrome (ed.), *Tales of Old Petworth.*
1985   P.A.L. Vine, *West Sussex Waterways.*
1989   M. Butlin, M. Luther & I. Warrell, *Turner at Petworth.*

(III) PERIODICALS

'The Waterways of Sussex', Roger Sellman (*Sussex County Magazine*, January–May 1935).
'The Third Earl of Egremont', Richard Walker (*Apollo,* January 1953).
'London's Lost Route to the Sea', P.A.L. Vine (*Country Life*, 27 March 1953).
'The Haslingbourne Navigation', G.D. Johnston (*Sussex Notes and Queries*, November 1964).
'A Forgotten Sussex Waterway', H.M. Peel (*Sussex Life*, April 1966).
'The Third Earl of Egremont and his Friends', Max Egremont (*Apollo*, October 1985).
'Spirited and Intelligent Farmers': The Arthur Youngs and the Board of Agriculture's Reports on Sussex, 1793 and 1808, John Farrant (*Sussex Archaeological Collections*, Vol. 130, 1992).

INDEX